Street by Street

CW00547514

MILTON KEYNES

BUCKINGHAM, LEIGHTON BUZZARD, NEWPORT PAGNELL, TOWCESTER

Aspley Guise, Bletchley, Cranfield, Linslade, Sherington, Silverstone, Stewkley, Stoke Bruerne, Winslow, Woburn

1st edition May 2001

© Automobile Association Developments Limited 2001

This product includes map data licensed from Ordnance Survey® with the permission of the Controller of Her Majesty's Stationery Office. © Crown copyright 2000. All rights reserved. Licence No: 399221.

Published by AA Publishing (a trading name of Automobile Association Developments Limited, whose registered office is Norfolk House, Priestley Road, Basingstoke, Hampshire, RG24 9NY. Registered number 1878835).

Mapping produced by the Cartographic Department of The Automobile Association.

A CIP Catalogue record for this book is available from the British Library.

Printed by GRAFIASA S.A., Porto, Portugal

The contents of this atlas are believed to be correct at the time of the latest revision. However, the publishers cannot be held responsible for loss occasioned to any person acting or refraining from action as a result of any material in this atlas, nor for any errors, omissions or changes in such material. The publishers would welcome information to correct any errors or omissions and to keep this atlas up to date. Please write to Publishing, The Automobile Association, Fanum House, Basing View, Basingstoke, Hampshire, RG21 4EA.

Ref: ML090

Key to map pages — ii-iii

Key to map symbols — iv-1

Enlarged scale pages — 2-3

Street by Street — 4-85

Index – towns & villages — 86

Index – streets — 87-97

Index – featured places — 97-98

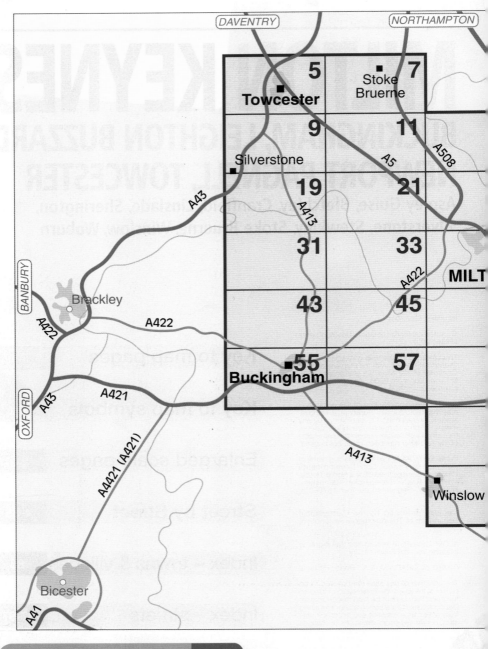

DAVENTRY

NORTHAMPTON

5	7
Towcester	Stoke Bruerne
9	11
Silverstone	A5 · A508
19	21
A43 · A413	
31	33
	A422 MILT
43	45
55	57
Buckingham	

BANBURY

Brackley

A422

A422

A421

OXFORD · A43

A4421 (A4421)

A413

Winslow

Bicester

A41

Enlarged scale pages 1:10,000 6.3 inches to 1 mile

| 0 | 1/4 | miles | 1/2 |
| 0 | 1/4 | 1/2 kilometres | 3/4 | 1 |

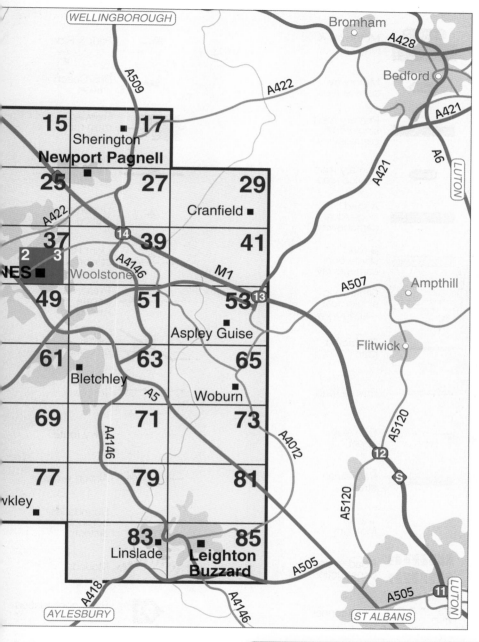

WELLINGBOROUGH

Bromham

A428

A422

Bedford

A421

A6

LUTON

15 **17**
Sherington
Newport Pagnell

25 **27** **29**
A422 Cranfield

A421

A421

37 **39** **41**
2 3
NES Woolstone
A4146 M1

A507 Ampthill

49 **51** **53**
Aspley Guise

Flitwick

61 **63** **65**
Bletchley A5 Woburn

69 **71** **73**
A4146 A4012

A5120

77 **79** **81**
vkley

A5120

83 **85**
Linslade **Leighton Buzzard**
A505

A418

AYLESBURY A4146 ST ALBANS LUTON

A505

3.6 inches to 1 mile **Scale of main map pages** **1:17,500**

0 ... 1/2 ... miles ... 1
0 ... 1/2 ... 1 ... kilometres ... 1 1/2

iv

Junction 9	Motorway & junction
Services	Motorway service area
	Primary road single/dual carriageway
Services	Primary road service area
	A road single/dual carriageway
	B road single/dual carriageway
	Other road single/dual carriageway
	Restricted road
	Private road
← ←	One way street
	Pedestrian street
	Track/ footpath
	Road under construction
} − − − − {	Road tunnel
P	Parking

P+	Park & Ride
	Bus/Coach station
⇌	Railway & main railway station
⇌	Railway & minor railway station
⊖	Underground station
⊖	Light Railway & station
+++++++++	Preserved private railway
LC	Level crossing
•—•—•—	Tramway
-----------	Ferry route
....	Airport runway
—••—••—••—	Boundaries- borough/ district
▼▼▼▼▼▼▼	Mounds
93	Page continuation 1:17,500
7	Page continuation to enlarged scale 1:10,000

River/canal,
lake, pier

Toilet with
disabled facilities

Aqueduct,
lock, weir

Petrol station

465
Winter Hill
Peak (with
height in
metres)

Public house

Beach

Post Office

Coniferous
woodland

Public library

Broadleaved
woodland

Tourist Information
Centre

Mixed
woodland

Castle

Park

Historic house/
building

Cemetery

Wakehurst
Place NT
National Trust
property

Built-up
area

Museum/
art gallery

Featured building

Church/chapel

City wall

Country park

A&E
Accident &
Emergency
hospital

Theatre/
performing arts

Toilet

Cinema

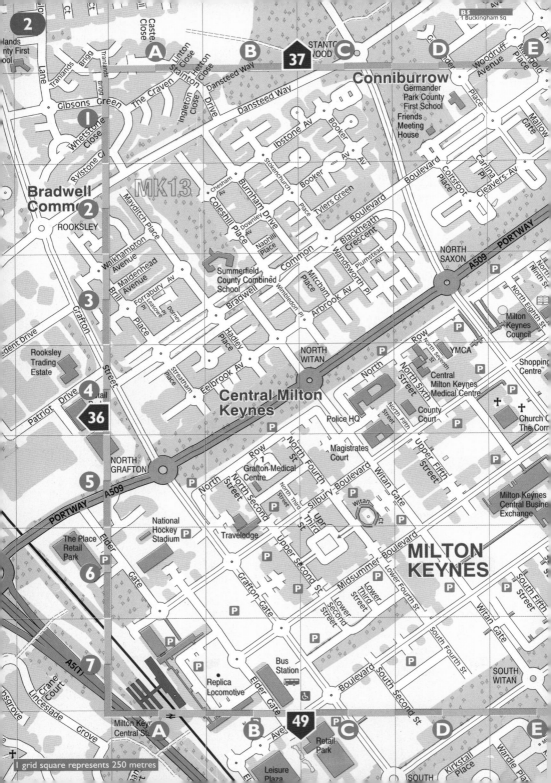

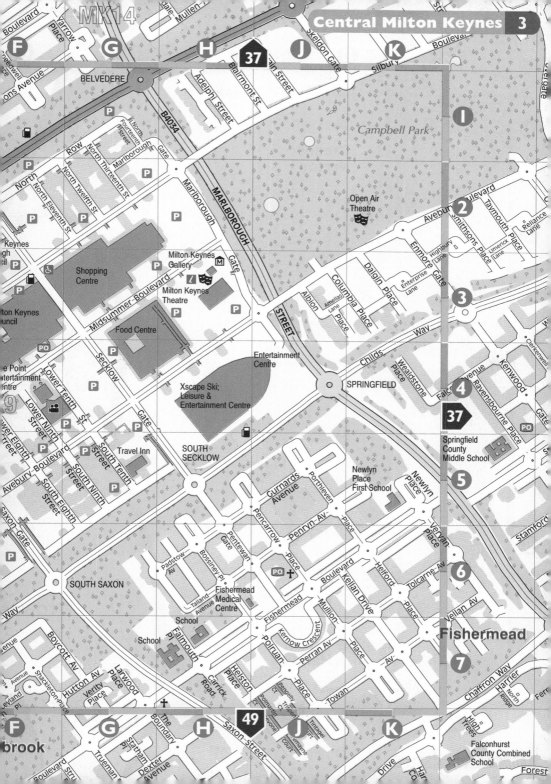

F G H J K

37

I

BELVEDERE

B4034

Campbell Park

Open Air
Theatre

2

Aveberry Boulevard
Tavmouth Place
Reliance Lane

MARLBOROUGH

North
Fourteenth Street
North Thirteenth St
Marlborough Gate
North Twelfth St
North Eleventh St
Marlborough Gate

Keynes

Row

North

Highbury Lane
Enmore Gate
Smithsons Place
Limerick Lane

Shopping
Centre

Milton Keynes
Gallery

Milton Keynes
Theatre

M

Dalgin place

Columbia Place

Enterprise
Lane

3

GH
ul

nton Keynes
uncil

Food Centre

Midsummer Boulevard

Albion

Amelias Lane

Way

Childs

Clerkenwell

e Point
ntertainment
ntre

9

Secklow

Lower Tenth

Entertainment
Centre

Xscape Ski;
Leisure &
Entertainment Centre

SPRINGFIELD

STREET

Wealdstone
Place

Falcon Avenue
Kenwood Gate
Ravensbourne Place

4

PO

37

Springfield
County
Middle School

Lower Ninth
Street

PO

Gate

SOUTH
SECKLOW

Newlyn
Place
First School

Newlyn
Place

Velvan
Place

5

er Eighth
Street

Avebury Boulevard

South Tenth
Street

Travel Inn

South Ninth
Street

South Eighth
Street

Gurnards
Avenue

Porthleven

Pencarrow
Gate

Penryn Av

Pentewan

Place

Helford

Tolcarne Av

6

Velvan Av

Stamford

Saxon Gate

SOUTH SAXON

Way

Boycott Av

Shackleton Place

Hutton Av

Larwood
Place

Verity
Place

Padstow
Av

Bossiney Pl

Talland
Avenue

Fishermead
Medical
Centre

School

School

Falmouth
Place

Carrick
Road

PO

Fishermead

Kelan Drive

Boulevard

Mullion

Kenow Crescent

Perran Av

Helston
Place

Poltuan
Place

Perran
Place

Towan
Av.

Dingelly
Triggel
Trannage
Court

Polmaise
Avenue

Chaffron Way

Harrier

North
Ridge

High
Trees

Ferr

Fishermead

7

F G H J K

49

brook

The Boundary

Statham
Place

Trueman
Av

Dexter
Avenue

Saxon Street

Harrier Drive

High

Falconhurst
County Combined
School

Forest

A   B   C   D   E

I

Blakesely

Falcon Manor
School

Greens Norton
Church of England
Primary School

Towcestrians
Sports Club

Bensham Road

Falcon View

Hill

New
Rd

School La

Cox
Gardens

Church View

Home Cl

Windmill Wy

PO

High Street

School
Close

Church
Close

Sycamore
Rd

Calvert Road

Calvert
Close

Bradden Wy

Road

Smithland
Ct

**Greens
Norton**

2

Bengal
View

Lodge
Farm

Bengal

Lane

Mill

Old Greens
Norton Road

Bengal

Lane

A5(T)

3

River Tove

NN12

Norton
Crs

Greenview

Cappenham
Close

Belle Baulk

Nene La

Ouse Lane

Tove

Brackley

Cemetery

4

Costwell
Farm

Hotel

Green Lane

Council
Offices

Wordsworth
Close

Shelley

Byron

Keats Drive

Tennyson Cl

Buckingham Dr

BUCK

Springfields

Primary
School

Hazel Crs

Hazel Crs

A43(T)

Sports
Centre

Dockwell Cl

Bramble Rd

Juniper Cl

Bath

Rowan

5

Mileoak
Farm

6

Park
Farm

Handley

TOWCE

Swinneyford
Farm

A   B

8

C   D   E

E5
1 Briary Cl
2 Redmoor

A43(T)

F3
1 The Ruins

F4
1 Hampton Ct Cl
2 Home Cl
3 St Georges Cl
4 Solly's Wy

Hulcote

Easton
Neston
House

Easton Neston
Park

Cappenham
Bridge

River To

6

Towcester
Race Cource

Tyrrell
Way

Surtees Way

Northampton Road

Hawthorn Drive

Clark Way

Graham
Hill Road

Hunt Close

Whittons Lane

Moat La

PO

Richmond Road

Donne Ho
hopping Cen

Park St

Chantry Lane

The Lindens

Bur Stable
Yard

Islington Rd

Sun St

Towcester
Infant School

St Lawrence
School

Towcester
Health
Centre

Vernon Road

Southgate
Drive

Willis Rd

Bairstow
Way

Sponnes Road

Marlow Rd

Park Vw. Rd

London Road A5(T)

Plank
Houses

Burcote Road

Robey Rd

Dryden
Road

Leeson Rd

Hicks Road

Piessey
Close

Jenkinson Road

Blackwell
Close

Brackencliffes

Hesketh Crs

Brick Kiln
Close

Woodburcote Way
Industrial Est

Towcester
Town F C

Hicks Road

Haresmoor
Drive

Oak Cl

Nightingale Drive

Wren Cl

Heron
Cl

Middle Rd

Dove Cl

Marble Rd

Linnet
Rd

Grafton Way

Lawrence Road South

Sycamore

Willow Rd

Heathencote

F
G
H
J
K

G3
1 The Lindens

**Wood
Burcot**

F6
1 Plover Cl
2 Robin Cl
3 Woodcroft Cl

F5
1 Baden Powell Crs

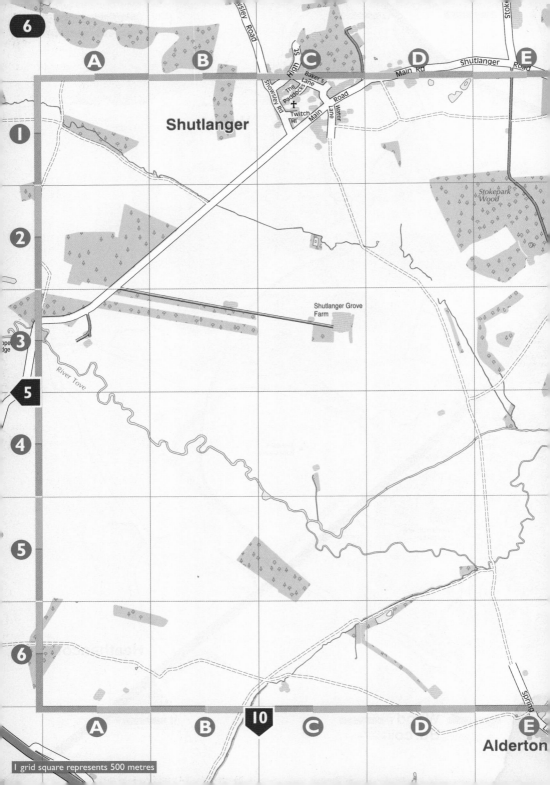

Mill Lane

Rookery Farm

Stoke Bruerne Cricket Club

F

G

Rookery Lane

A508

H

Ashton Road

J

K

Manor Farm

Ashton C of E Primary School

Museum

Chapel La

M

Stoke Bruerne C of E Primary School

Bakers Lane

PH

Stoke Bruerne

Stoke Road

Roade Hill

St Michael

1

Ashton

2

Grand Union Canal Wk

Rectory Farm

3

Bozenham

Stoke Park Pavilions

Grand Union Canal

Grand Union Canal Walk

4

NORTHAMPTON ROAD

5

Pury Road

Pury Rd

A508

Northamptonshire Countr

6

Brick Kiln Farm

Bozenham Mill Lane

F

G

H

II

J

K

The Lane

Church Road

PH

Grafton Regis

8

A **B** **C** **D** **E**

Handley

4

Park Farm

Swinneyford Farm

A6
1 Stocks HI

1

2

A43(T)

Bu
Fa

3

Silverstone
Fields Farm

4

Pits Farm

A43(T)

A413

Lordsf
Farm

5

6

A43(T)

BRACKLEY ROAD

Kingsley
Road

London

Hillside Av

Little

Silson
Surgery

Church

Street

Whittlebury   Road

Dove's
Farm

Ch

The
Home

Silverstone

Chapel

Oak Dr

Hall

FOO

the stable

PO

Old

Mutsw

Austins Pl

TOWCESTER ROAD

A **B** **18** **C** **D** **E**

Junior

High

Green

Whitt

1 grid square represents 500 metres

F G H 5 J K

Wood Burcote

I

2

3

Grafton Way

Careys Road

Scriveners Lane

Pury End

10

The Green

Lower Street

PO

K Lane

4 F

Grafton Way

Kings Lane

Grafton Way

Porterswood Farm

5

Grafton

Park Farm

TOWCESTER ROAD

Whittlebury

The Crescent

A413

Sholebroke Lodge

6

F G H 19 J K

Whittlebury
Church of England
Primary School

KS
1 Manor Wy
2 School La
3 Woodville Crs

Farm

F

G

H

7

J

K

Bozenham Mill

The Lane

PH Church Road

Grafton Regis

Grafton Lodge

I

Grand Union Canal Walk

2

NORTHAMPTON ROAD A508

3

Grafton Fields

Grand

12

Canal

4

Queens Oak Farm

Potterspury Lodge School

Grafton Way

Grafton Way

Moor End

Gavs

Moorend Road

Highcroft Cl

Lime Rd 1

Grafton Way

Village Cl

Hesketh 3 2

Brownsfield Road

Grafton Road

Orchard Cl

5

PO

Warren Road

Yardley Gobion C of E Primary School

Hortonsfield Rd

Eastfield

Yardley Gobion

Grafton Way

6

A5(T)

F

G

H

21

J

K

Yardley Road

Beech House Farm

slade

12

A   B   C   D   E

Hun End

Milton Keynes Boundary Walk

Hanslope Circular Ride

Northamptonshire

Grand Union Canal Walk

1

2

Fiery Furze

3

Lincoln Lodge

11

Grand Union Canal

Old Wharf Farm

River Tove

4

Milford Leys Farm

Grafton Road

Road

Brownsfield Rd

5

Pleasant

PO

High St

Orchard

Cl

Warren Road

Chestnut Rd

Hortonsfield Rd

Bridge Rd

Eastfield Crs

Isworth Farm

Grand Union Canal Walk

Northamptonshire

Milton Keynes

6

Yardley Road

NORTHAMPTON ROAD A508

A   B   **22**   C   D   E

Grand Union Canal

1 grid square represents 500 metres

Beech House Farm

Cheley Well

F G H J K

Williams Cl
Green End
Kittlewants
Eastfield
Juduit
Combined School
Wine Dard
Western Dr
Warwick Rd
Drive
Adene Rd
Western Dr
Gold St
Keswick Rd
PO
Nevill Pl
Doctors Surg
High St
St James Close
Newport Road
The
Manor Green End
Weavers
Weavers
Park Road

I

2

Ivy Farm

3

Manor Farm

14

4

Bullington End

Hanslope Circular

Hanslope Lodge

5

Castlethorpe Road

Hanslope Road

Bullington End Road

Lodge Court
Farm

Thrupp Cl

First School

North St
North St
South St
North St
South St
Bens School
PO
New Rd
Prospect Pl

6

Wolverton Road

Station Road
The Chequers
Shepperton Close

Woad

Pike's Farm

J6
1 Hemingway Cl

K6
1 Auden Cl
2 Thomas Dr

F   G   Hringham   J   K

Gayhurst

Tyringham Health Clinic

Tyringham Hall

Back

Fences   Three Shires Way   Lane

I

B526

Gayhurst House

2

Quarry Hall Farm

3

Shires Way

16

Hoo Wood

Mill Farm

River Great Ouse

4

Kickle's Farm

5

M1

Flora Thompson Drive

Larkin Cl

Heaney

Housman

Little Linford

Elliot Cl

Westoun Lane

Shakespeare Cl

Carroll Cl

Christie Cl

Herriot

Swift

Scott Cl

6

Sitwell Cl

Spark Way

Wordsworth

Lewis Cl

Shaw

Portfields Combined School

Westbury Lane

Newbolt Cl

Yeats Cl

Owen

Hughes

Avenue

F   G   H   25   J   K

Thyme

Pennycress Way

Sorrell Dr

Kingsley

Marlow Dr

Byron Cl

Downing

Tennyson

Ash Hill Road

Kipling Dr

Carlile

Keats

Spencer Cl

Avenue

Portfields Rd

Little Linford

Burns

Cooper

Shelley Cl

C6
1 Union St

A   B   C   D   E

Shires Way
Lane
Fences Farm

1

Baker's Farm

Village Close

Water
Lane
Water   Lane

High   Street

Knoll Cl

Leys View
PO

Gallards
Farm

2

3

B526

15

Ouse

Sherington
Bridge

Lathbury

Bridge House

Sherington   Road

4

Church Lane
Inn Farm
Court

NORTHAMPTON   ROAD

River Great Ouse

Church La
Lathbury
Park

Kickle's Farm

5

Sherington   Road

Bury
Field

B526

6

Swift
ott Dr

Woad
Farm

Westbury Lane

Lakes Lane

NEWPORT
PAGNELL

High St
Shelley
Close
Dennyson
Rd

Cowper
Dr

Westbury
Close

A

Queens Av

B

Dovecote

Sheppards
Close

Sheppards
PO

Newport
Pagnell
Medical Ce

Newport
Clinic/nutri
1centre

North
Square

Mill St

26

PO

HIGH   STREET

Tickford
Abbey

North
Square

St
JOHN
ST

ST   JOHN
ST

Silver St

Waterhouse

C

River
Side

Ousebank

Cem

Lagonda
Close

Priory
Close

Keynes Cl

Milton
Dr

Carlton Cl

D

Chichley St

TICKFORD   STREET

Tickford
End

E

1 grid square represents 500 metres

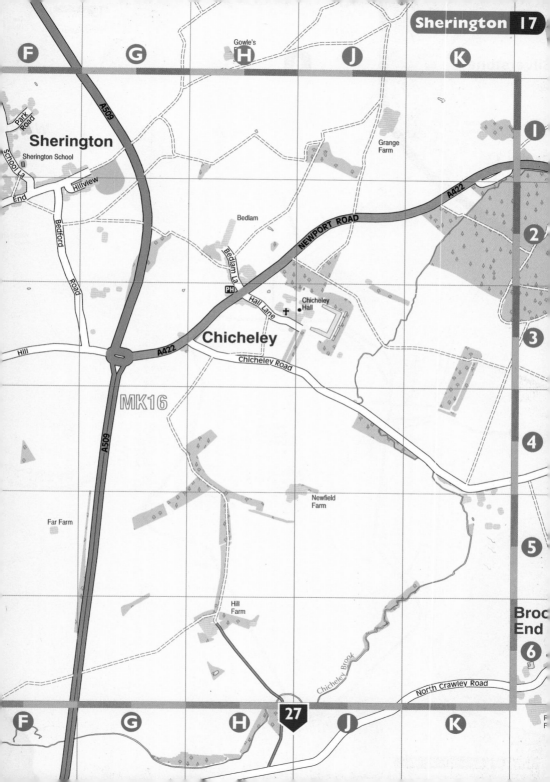

18

Silverstone

Little
Silson
Surgery

A   **B**   **8**   **C**   **D**   **E**

Whittlebury Road

AI
1 Brabham Cl
2 Home Cl
3 Walnut Cl
4 The Woodlands

The
Home F

I

Cattle
End

Junior
School

Foxhole
Copse

Whittle

West Park
Farm

2
3(T)

BRACKLEY ROAD

TOWCESTER ROAD

Wild
Wood

Cheese
Copse

3

Chapel
Copse

Gol

4

Silverstone
Motor Racing
Circuit

Northamptonshire County
Buckinghamshire County

5

Becketts
Corner

6

A   **B**   **30**   **C**   **D**   **E**

Silverstone
Golf Club

1 grid square represents 500 metres

A43
TOWCE
Crescent
F
G
H
9
J
K

Whittlebury
Church of England
Primary School

I

Old Tun
Copse

HIGH STREET

Lodge Park
Park Close
Road

2

Buckingham Thick
Copse

Coldthorn

Northamptonsh

Buckingham

3

Linshire Copse

20

Birch Copses

Home Farm

4

A413

Lovel
Wood

5

Boundary
Farm

Shrine's
Wood

6

A413

F
Hall
Farm

G

H

31

J

K

Keyes Farm

Lillingstone

PO

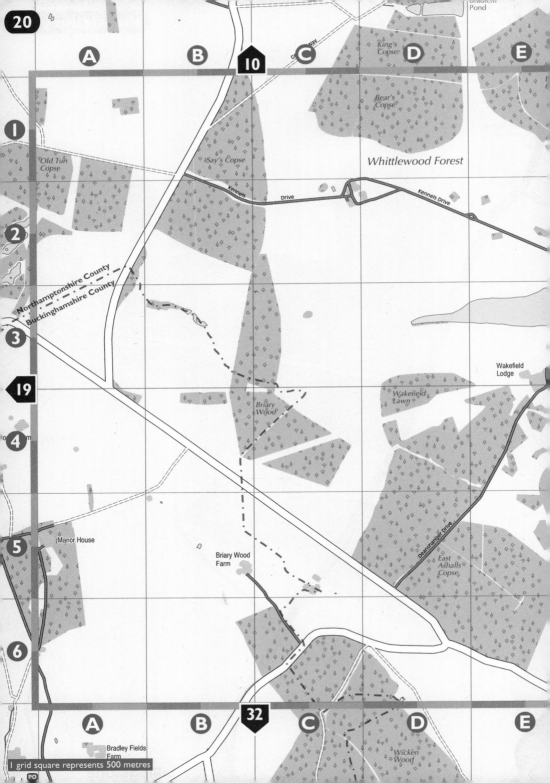

A   **B**   10   **C**   **D**   **E**

Bradden Pond

Coffee Way

King's Copse

Bear's Copse

I

Old Tun Copse

Say's Copse

Whittlewood Forest

Kennels   Drive   Kennels Drive

2

Northamptonshire County
Buckinghamshire County

3

Wakefield Lodge

19

Wakefield Lawn

Briary Wood

4

Dearshanger Drive

5

Manor House

East Ashalls Copse

Briary Wood Farm

6

A   **B**   32   **C**   **D**   **E**

Bradley Fields Farm

Wicken Wood

I grid square represents 500 metres

PO

Wolverton Road

F G H 13 J K

Castlethorpe

Pike's Farm

I

Lodge Farm Industrial Estate

Lodge Farm

2

The Priory

River Tove

The Green

Hav

MK19

3

Cosgrove Primary School

Lodge Road

Park Cl The Gn

The stocks

Main St

Lock La

The Gn

Cosgrove Leisure Park

24

4

Grafton Way

Ouse Valley Park

Manor Farm

Colts Holm

5

Dickens Rd

Old Wolverton

Great Ouse

Milton Keynes Boundary Walk

Dean's Road

Canons Road

Grand Union Canal Walk

Old Wolverton

Longville

N Buckinghamshire W

Trinity Rd

Manor Rd Carton Rd

The Meacham Clinic

Stratford Road

Cambridge St

Church

6

Buckingham St

mptonshire County

River Great Ouse

Milton Keynes

Wyvern County First School

Anson Rd

Slated RW

MK12

35

Radcliffe School

Aylesbury Street West

Peel Rd

Eton Rd

Windsor St

Oxford St

Aylesbury St

F G H 35 J K

Street

Ryeland

Breton

A5

Stratford Road

Hamett Dr

Turneys Dr

PO

Great Monks Street

Western Road

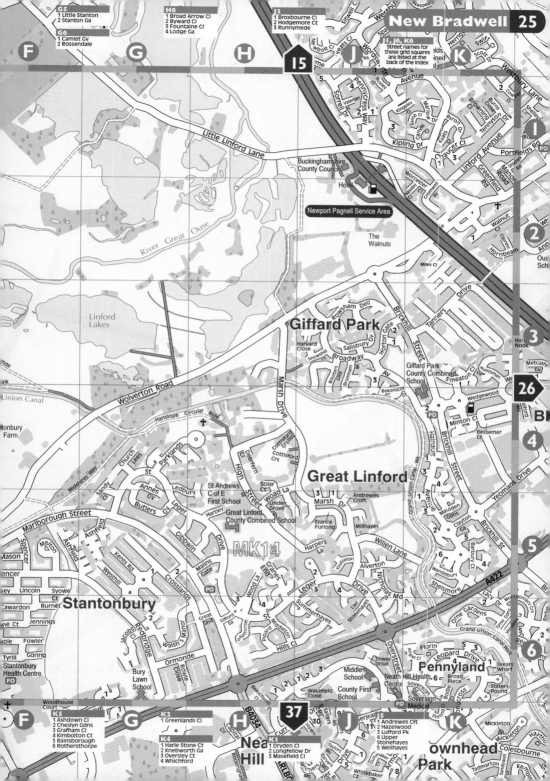

F G H 17 Chichel Brook J North Cr K Road

I

2

Tickford Lodge
Farm

3

Tickford Park
Farm 28

Tickford
Park 4

Wood End Lane

Cranfield Road

Willow Close

PH

Moulsoe

Newport Road ✝ 5

6

Junction 14 39

F Hermitage G H J K
Farm

A509

A B C D E

I

Rectory
Farm

Murtla
Farm

2

Hurstend
Farm

**Hurst
End**

Milton Keynes Boundary Walk

Royce
Road

Wharley End

The Drive

West Road

Lanchest

3

27

Moulsoe
Old
Wood

The
Cottage

4

Wharley
End Farm

Wood End
Farm

Milton Keynes
Bedfordshire County

Technology
Park

5

Lower
Wood

6

Leys
Farm

Milton Keynes Boundary Walk

1 grid square represents 500 metres

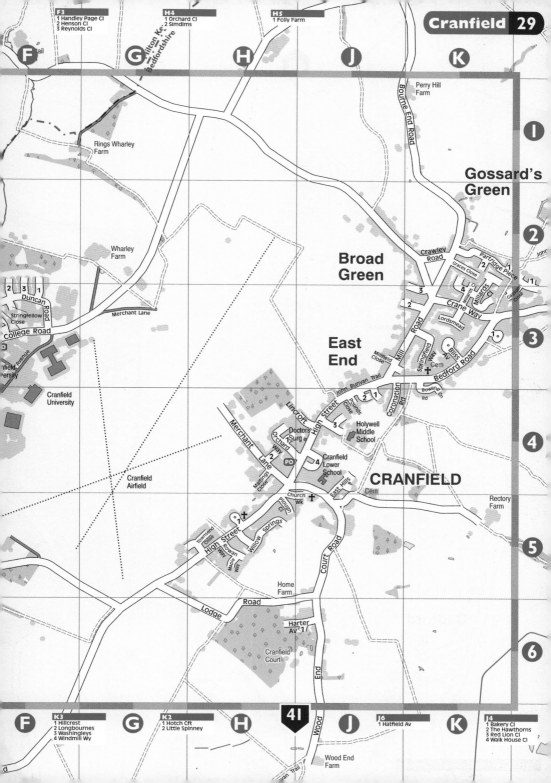

F3
1 Handley Page Cl
2 Henson Cl
3 Reynolds Cl

H4
1 Orchard Cl
2 Simdims

H5
1 Folly Farm

F G H J K

Milton Ke...
Bedfordshire

Perry Hill
Farm

Rings Wharley
Farm

Gossard's Green

I

Wharley
Farm

2

Broad Green

Crawley
Road

Graces Close

Partridge Piece

John...

2

Millards Cl

Camden Close

3

4

Millards Cl

Crane Way

2

Lordsmead

3

Stringfellow
Close

Duncan Road

2 3 1

College Road

Merchant Lane

Springfield Way

Mill Road

Cem

Bliss Cl

1

Bowling Grn Rd

Bedford Road

...field Avenue

...University

East End

Millfield Close

John Bunyan Trail

Coronation Rd

Bowling Gn Rd

Cranfield
University

Lincroft

High Street

Pounds Close

2 1

1

Merchant Lane

Doctors Surg

3

Holywell
Middle
School

Cranfield
Airfield

Orchard Way

2

PO

4

Cranfield
Lower
School

East Hills

CRANFIELD

Maltings Close

Church Wk

Cem

Rectory
Farm

Church Wk

High Street

Townsend Close

Rowan Way

Moon Way

Plough Cl

Willow Springs

Court Road

4

5

Lodge Road

Home
Farm

Harter Av

1

End

Wood

6

Cranfield
Court

41

K3
1 Hillcrest
2 Longbournes
3 Washingleys
4 Windmill Wy

K2
1 Hotch Cft
2 Little Spinney

J6
1 Hatfield Av

J4
1 Bakery Cl
2 The Hawthorns
3 Red Lion Cl
4 Walk House Cl

Wood End
Farm

Bunyan Trail

F   G   H   **19**   J   K

I

2

3

32

4

5

6

Hatch-hill Farm

Keyes Farm

Lillingstone Lovell

Church Lane

Brookside

PO

A413

A413

Lillingstone Dayrell

Tile House Farm

Bycell Road

Whitehouse

Lillingstone House

Stockholt Farm

F   G   H   **43**   J   K

Cedars Close

Chapel Lane

Akeley

C of E School

Church

STREET

32

Ⓐ 　　　Ⓑ 　20　Ⓒ 　　　Ⓓ 　　　Ⓔ

PO

Brookside

Bradley Fields
Farm

Wicken
Wood

Ⓘ

2

Leckhampstead
Wood

3

31

Hill Farm

Northamptonshire County
Buckinghamshire County

4

5

Park
Copse

6

Lodge
Farm

44

Church
End

W. Road

Ⓐ 　　　Ⓑ 　44　Ⓒ 　　　Ⓓ 　　　Ⓔ

1 grid square represents 500 metres

F G H **21** J K

I

Hanger Lodge

Folly Fields Farm

arm

2

Puxley Road

Glebe

High View

Road

Hayes R

Folly Road

Westfield Avenue

Ridgmont Way

North Way

Elm Drive

Puxley Road

The Riding

Porter's Close

Ridgmont Little

Springfield Gdns

Boswell La

London Lane

Hayes Road

Deanshanger

Brookway

High Street

3

PO

Church Lane

Patrick's Lane

The Green

34

Buckingham

Pound Close

St John's Lane

Church Close

Deanshanger Road

The Beeches

Deanshanger Primary School

4

Cross Tree Road

Wicken

Road

Dagnall Farm

5

Sparrow Lodge

6

Akeley Wood Junior School

Wicken Park

Akeley Wood

Mount Mill Farm

F G H **45** J K

Wicken P

F2
1 The Carne

F3
1 Stotfold Ct

G2
1 Cottesloe Ct
2 Flitton Ct
3 Lamva Ct

The Meacham Clinic

Stratford

MK12

Wyvern County First School

Radcliffe School

Aylesbury street West

Anson Road

Jersey

Peel Rd

Eton Crs

Windsor St

Western Road

Oxford St

Buckingham

Aylesbury

Wolver Sports Club

Osbourne Pl

Wolverton

Cemetery

Furze Wy

Stratford Road

Harnett Dr

Turneys Dr

PO

Blacknill Dr

Wolverton Mill

Featherstone Rd

Street

Woburn

Frank Atter Croft

Marron Lane

Middle School

Wolverton Hlth Centre & Day Hosp

Gloucester

Ryeland

Breton Road

Boundary Crs

Woodside

Debbs Close

Mallards Crt

Frampton Av

Ancell Rd

Essendon Court

Cresslow

Galley Hl

Murley

Eleanor

Mill Sq

Mill Ct

Ridgeway

Oxman La

Sowerman

Harvester

Bee

Cleeman

Thresher

Combined School

Great Field La

Field La

Ardwell

Monks Lane

Street

Middle School

PO

Greenleys Ct

Greenleys

Milton Keynes Rugby Club

Plowman Close

Tillman Close

Henders

Hastings

Hale Av

Queen

Galley Hl

Cem

Galley Hl

Buckley Court

PO

Barford

Ridgeway

Woolmans

Sidlaw Ct

Woolmans

Moorfoot

Fullers Slade

A5(T)

Millers Way

Rovers Crt

Hodge Lea La

Golspie Crt

Blenheim Av

Avenue

Latimer

Ridgeway

Blackdown

Pentlands

Malvern Dr

Sladers Lane

Welland

Shepherds

West Slade Lane

Shearmans

Millers Way

Bellweth

Burners Lane

Burners Lane South

Potters La

Strathaven Pl

Dalt

Kildorran

Golf Course

Tudor Gdns

MK11

Pitfield

Kiln Farm Industrial Estate

Carters Lane

Brunleys

Pitfield

Watling Street

In Buckinghamshire Way

Tilers Road

Brick Close

Centurion Ct

Monks Way

Atherstone

Samtawill

Badgemore Ct

Fairways

The Westcliffe

Thorncliffe

Watling

Two Mil

ver Weald

Calverton

iddle Weald

Calverton Lane

Calverton Lane

Common Farm

36

2

3

4

5

6

F

G

H

J

K

K5
1 Belmont Ct
2 Harborne Ct

J2
1 Akerman Cl
2 Buckman Cl
3 Catchpole Cl
4 Cotman Cl
5 Freeman Cl
6 Herdman Cl

G3
1 Galley Hl

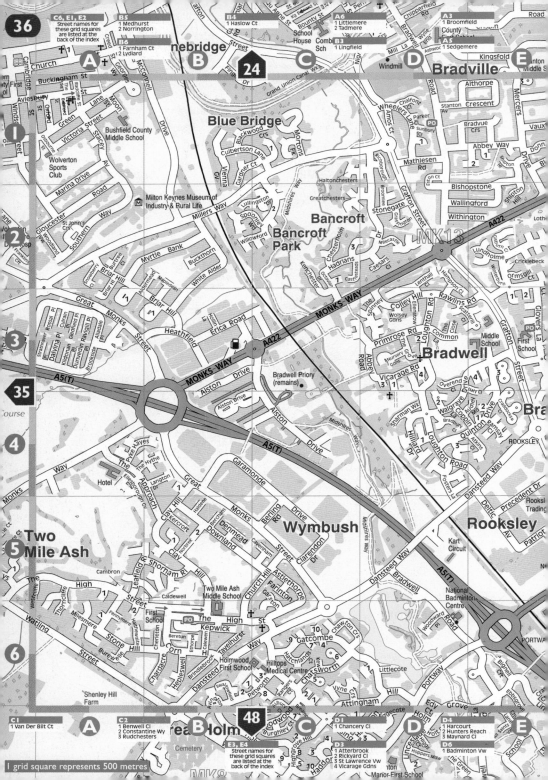

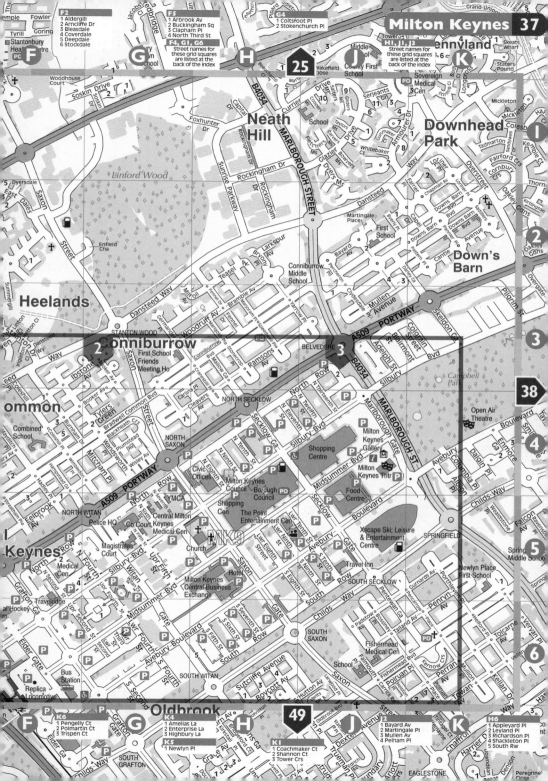

40

A   B   **28**   C   D   E

Leys Farm

Milton Keynes Boundary Walk

1

Broughton Grounds

2

Broughton Barn Cottage

Whitsundoles Farm

Milton Keynes Boundary Walk

Cran

Cranfield Road

3

39

Broughton Road

Brittons Lane

Mill Lane

4

Salford

Wavendon Road

5

A421

6

A421

M1

A421

Lower End

Crow Lane

Cranfield Road

A   B   Lower Road   **52**   C   D   E

Wavendon House Drive

Wavendon

Crabtree Farm

1 grid square represents 500 metres

F G H **29** J K

Cranfield
Court

Wood End

I

Wood End
Farm

John Bunyan Trail

Holcotmoors
Farm

Holcot
Wood

2

3

John Bunyan Trail

North
Farm

4

Rooktree
Farm

Brogborough
Manor Farm

5

Hulcote

Aspley
Hall

Hulcote
Farm

Br

Highfield
Farm

Club
House

Hill
Crescent

PO

6

Highfield
Crescent

Ridgway Road

Salford Rd

53

F A421 G H J K

BEDFORD ROAD

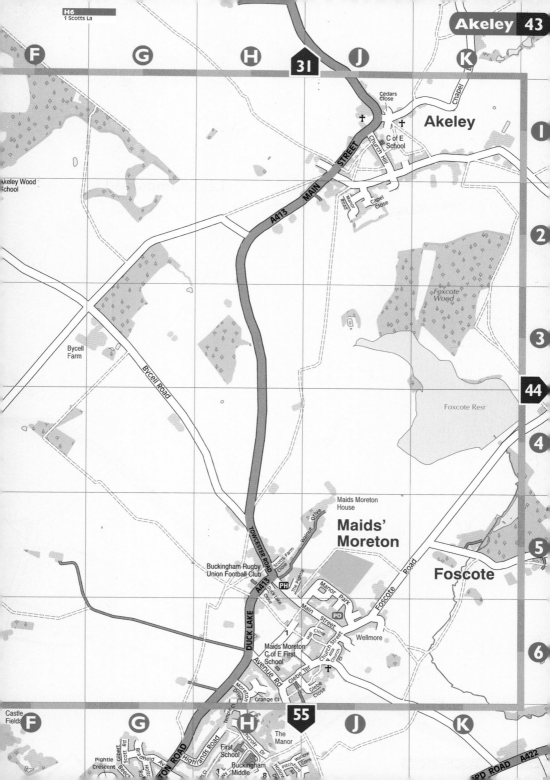

F Akeley Wood School

Wicken Park

Akeley Wood

G

H

33

A422

J

K

Mount Mill Farm

I

Northamptonshire County

Buckinghamshire County

2

Wicken Park Road

Little Hill Farm

3

46

Blackfields Farm

4

Cattleford Brige

† Thornton College

Thornton

5

Thornton Hall

6

F

G

H

57

J

K

Tyrellcote Farm

46

A   B   **34** Mill Farm   C   D   E

Milton Keynes
Buckinghamshire County

1

Hill Farm

2

✝

Thornton Road

Main Street

Rimers Close

Watery Lane

Beachampton

3

45

Beachampton Grove

lds Farm

4

5

Great Wood

Potash Farm

6

Furzenfield Farm

A   Cowper Wood   B   **58**   C   D   E

Tyrellcote Farm

I grid square represents 500 metres

Calver

F G H 35 J
Common
Farm
K

Calverton Lane

I

**Upper
Weald**

Whitehouse
Farm

North Buckinghamshire Way

2

3

Milton Keynes

Boundary Wk

Shenley Dens
Farm

48

Grove
Farm

4

Milton Keynes Boundary Walk

The
Oaks

Milton Keynes Boundary Wk

Milton Keynes

Buckinghamshire County

Oakhill
Wood

5

6

Stratford

F G H 59 J K

Road

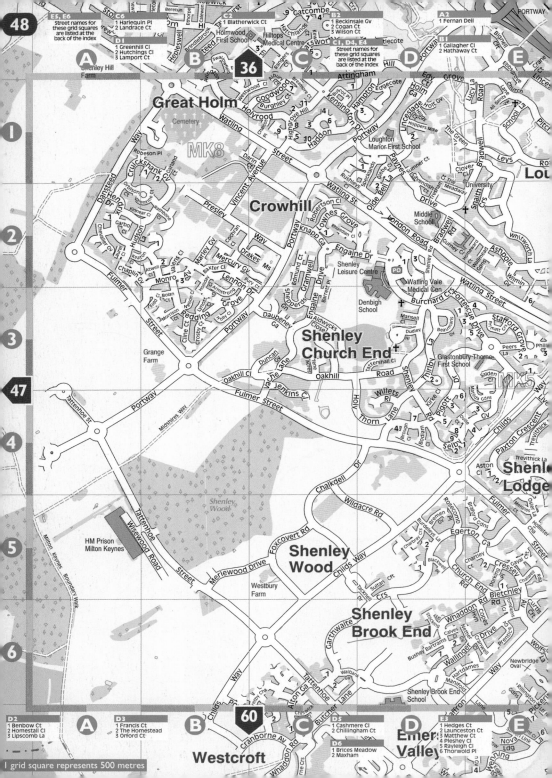

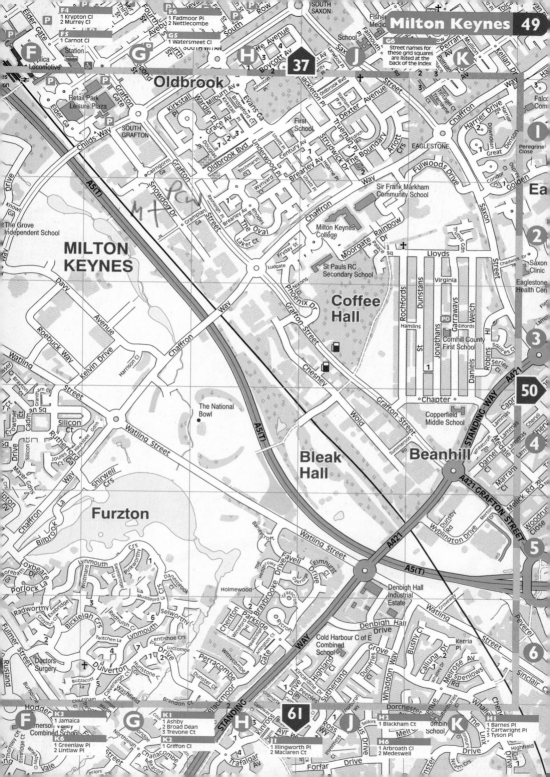

F · G · H · J · K

43

Wellmore

Maids Moreton C of E First School

STRATFORD ROAD A4

Old Mill House

1

2

River Great Ouse

56

Manor Farm

3

Bourton Road

4

A421

5

6

Bourton

The Manor

First School

Buckingham Middle School

Page Hill

Busby Av

Avenue

Community Hospital

Masonic House Surg

Buckingham Town Council

Verney Close Family Practice

Portfield Close

Buckingham Town Football Club

County Middle School

Buckingham School

Royal Latin School

The Swan Pool & Leisure Centre

Buckingham University

Burleigh Piece

Burleigh Piece

Jarman Close

Bourton Meadow County Combined School

WEST STREET

HIGH ST

MORETON ROAD

STRATFORD ROAD

A422

A413

Addington Rd

Overn Crescent

Western Avenue

Dragon Gallery

Stowe Rise

Grenville Rd

Willow Drive

Lime Avenue

Benthill Farm

Hillcrest Rise

Top Angel

Great Slade

Middle Slade

Ball Moor

Hotel

LONDON

A413

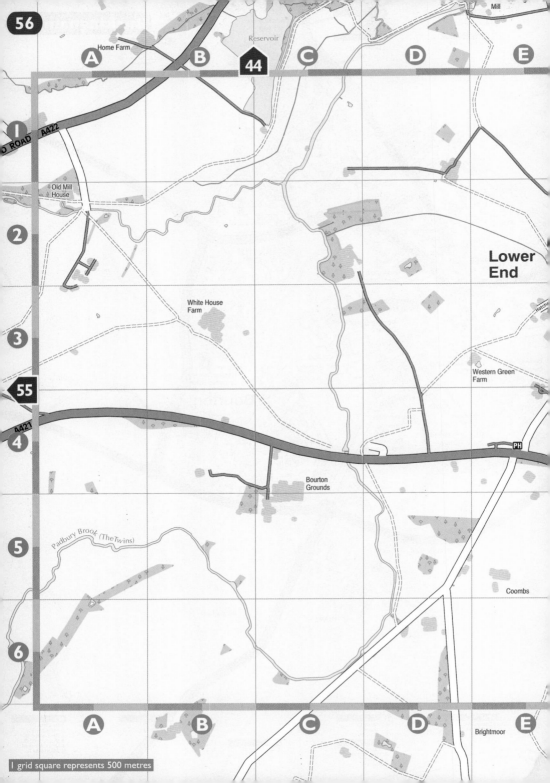

56

A B 44 C D E

Home Farm
Reservoir
Mill

I
D ROAD A422
Old Mill
House

2

Lower
End

White House
Farm

3

Hatch

55

Western Green
Farm

A421

4
PH

Bourton
Grounds

Padbury Brook (The Twins)

5

Coombs

6

Brightmoor

A B C D E

I grid square represents 500 metres

F   G   H   45   J   K

Tyrellcote Farm

I

Langbridge Farm

2

Thornborough

3

Street

Palmers Moor

Chapel La

High Street

Thornborough First School

Church Lane

The Gn

PO   Nash   Road

Thornhill

58

Shelspit Farms

4

Street

Bridge

The Folly

A421

Priory Farm

5

Mangland Farm

Pilch Lane

6

Pilch Lane

Singleborough

F   G   H   J   K

Pilch Farm

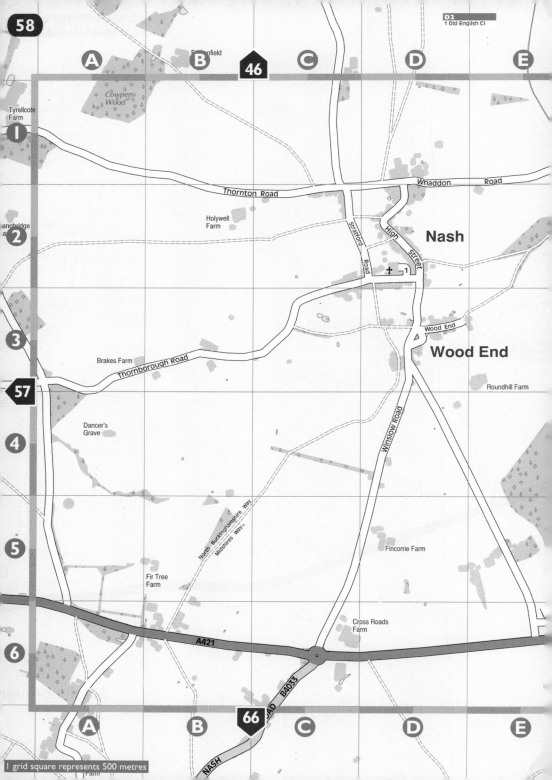

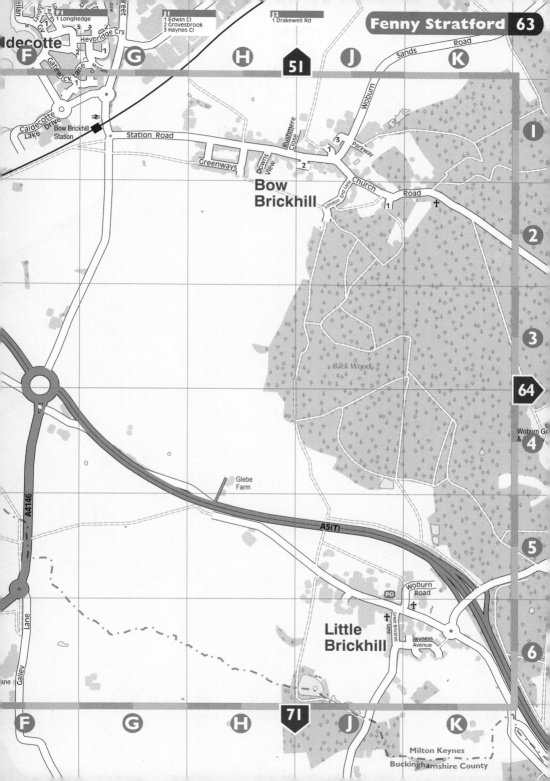

F **G** **H** **J** **K**

Idecotte

F1
1 Longhedge

J1
1 Edwin Cl
2 Grovesbrook
3 Haynes Cl

J2
1 Drakewell Rd

Heybridge Crs

Sands   Road

Gatewick Lane

Mortain Cl

51

I

Caldecotte
Lake

Bow Brickhill
Station

Station Road

Greenways

Downs
View

Rushmere Close

London End Lane

Woburn

Parkway

Church   Road

**Bow
Brickhill**

✝

2

A4146

Back Wood

3

64

Woburn Go
&

4

Glebe
Farm

A5(T)

Galley   Lane

5

Woburn
Road

PO

**Little
Brickhill**

✝

Great Brickhill   Lane

✝

Wyness
Avenue

6

71

Milton Keynes
Buckinghamshire County

64

A **B** **C** **D** **E**

Wavendon
Wood

Aspley
Heath

52

Milton Keynes Boundary Walk

Silverbirches Lane

Milton Keynes
Bedfordshire County

Heath Lane

Church Road

North Dr

Holly
Walk

Narrow Lane

Path

Sandy

Fernwood
School

WOBURN

Aspley
Wood

I

Old
Wavendon
Heath

ROAD

2

Milton Keynes Boundary Walk

New
Wavendon
Heath

3

63

Bell's
Cops

Hundreds
Farm

Woburn Golf
& Country Club

4

Charle
Wood

Little
Brickhill
Copse

5

Lowe's
Wood

Job's
Farm

6

Greensand Ridge Walk

Milton Keynes Boundary Walk

UG

A **B** **72** **C** **D** **E**

Buttermilk
Wood

Greensand Ridge Walk

I grid square represents 500 metres

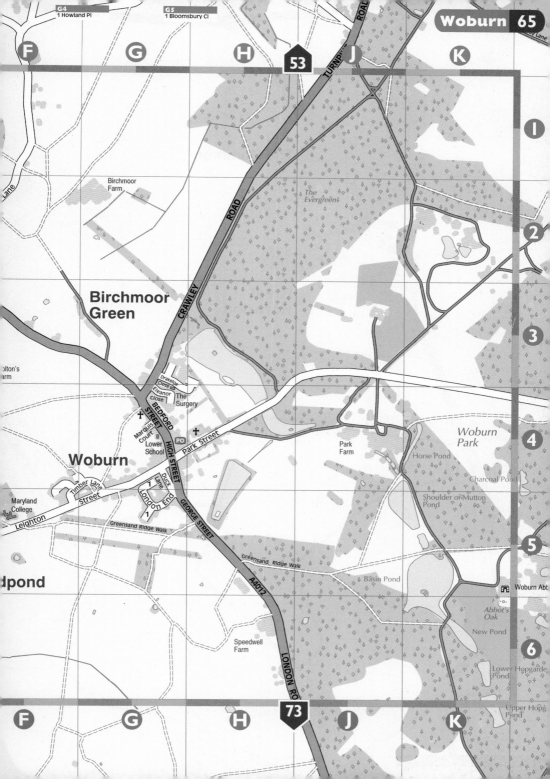

A   B   58   C   D   E

1

Laurel
Farm

The Common

NASH   ROAD   B4053

THE GREEN

2

Great
Horwood
School

School
End

HIGH ST

PO

Singleborough La

Little   Horwood   Road   Sunnyhill

Wheathouse
Copse

Willow
Rd

Western
The Cl
Road

Townsend
Cottages

Spring
Lane

Wigwell
Gdns

Spring Cl

Great
Horwood

3

Spring
Lane

Greenway

WINSLOW ROAD

B4033

Greenway
Farm

4

Greenway
Farm

Winslow

5

The
Hollows

GREAT

6

HORWOOD

edfield

A   B   74   C   D   E

ROAD

Warren Farm

Warren Road

F G H 59 J K

Fernfield Farm

Stearthill Farm

Chase Farm

Manor

Midshires Way

Norbury Coppice

Wood End

Crabtree Farm

Wood End

Little Horwood

rsley

Road

68

Spring Grove Farm

Horwood House

Midshires Way

Station Road

Lowergrove Farm

Whaddon

Tweedale Close

The Lane

F G H 75 J K

1
2
3
4
5
6

68

A B **60** C D E

I

Chase
Farm

Lower Salden
Farm

Bletchley Leys
Farm

Leys

Midshires Way

2

Salden
Wood

3

67

Springfield Farm

4

Cowpasture
Farm

5

Salden

MI

6

Whaddon Road

Tweedale Close

The Lane

A B **76** C D E

Cooks Lane

D
F

I grid square represents 500 metres

F2
1 Lilac Cl
2 Orchard Cl

G1
1 Red House Cl

G2
1 The Chase
2 Church End

F G H **61** J K

Milton Keynes
Buckinghamshire County

Milton Keynes Boundary Wk

I

2

Applecroft

Bletchley Road

Bonnards Rd

Berry Way

Green Way

Whaddon

PO

Betty's Cl

Paradise

Manor Rd

Bay Tree Cl

London End

Fire Ln

Home Farm

The Slade

St. Faith's Cl

Stoke Road

3

Westbrook

Cobb Hall

Ivy La

Warners Road

Brookfield Road

Sportfield

Newton
Longville

Borough Farm

70

Rectory Farm

4

Yew Tree Cl

School Drive

Crofts

Elm Cl

Chestnut La

Bletchley Road

Pond Cl

End

Drovers Wy

Drayton Road

5

Newton Road

Drayton Crossroad Farm

6

Dorcas Farm

Lodge
Industrial
Centre

Prospect Cl

Highw

Drayton Parslow

Little
Brickh

63

F G H J K

1 Home Farm La

Lane

I

Milton Keynes
Buckinghamshire County

2

Park
Farm

Duncombe
Wood

ld Farm

Milton Keynes Boundary Wlk

Galley Lane

Green End

3

Cemetery

Rectory
Farm

Great
Brickhill
Cricket Club

Rotten Row

High Ash C of E
Combined School

Milton Keynes

Boundary Walk

72

Lower Way

Upper Way

Naisby
Drive

Pound Hill

**Great
Brickhill**

Warners Close

4

Lower Rectory
Farm

Way

Knights
Close

Heath Road

PH

Stoke Lane

Holts
Green

Cuff Lane

Duck
End

Ivy Lane
Farm

5

Ivy Lane

Paper
Mill

Greensand Ridge Walk

6 St
Co

F G H J K

79

Bragenham Lane

Bragenham

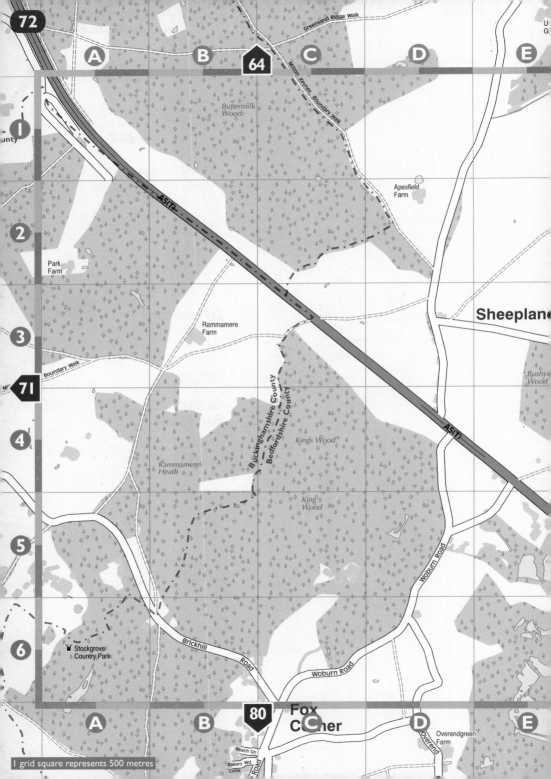

72

A B **64** C D E

Greensand Ridge Walk

Milton Keynes Boundary Walk

1

County

Buttermilk Wood

Apesfield Farm

A5(T)

2

Park Farm

Sheeplane

3

Rammamere Farm

Boundary Walk

Bushy Wood

71

Mi

4

Buckinghamshire County

Bedfordshire County

Kings Wood

Rammamere Heath

King's Wood

A5(T)

5

Woburn Road

6

Stockgrove Country Park

Brickhill Road

Woburn Road

A B **80** C D E

Fox Corner

Overendgreen Farm

Overend

Reach Gn

Bakers Wd Close

Road

1 grid square represents 500 metres

F G H 65 J K

New Pond

Lower Hopgarde Pond

Upper Hopg Pond

I

2

Speedwell Farm

Speedwell Belt

LONDON ROAD

A4012

LONDON ROAD

3

Milton Lodge

Old Farm

Battlesden Avenue

Avenue

4

Hill Farm

Hunge Wood

5

Manor Farm

Potsgrove

Home Wood

Battlesden

6

Battlesden Park

F G H 81 J K

E

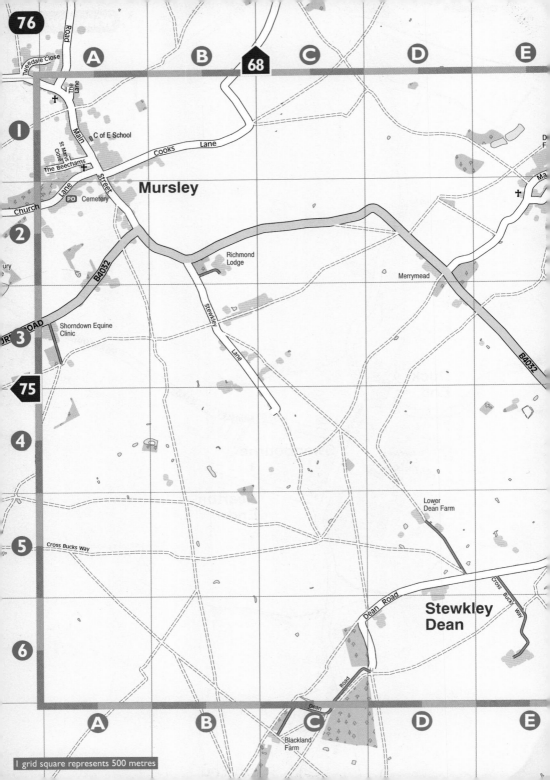

A   B   68   C   D   E

Tweedale Close

The Lane

Road

†

C of E School

Main

St Mary's Close

The Beechams †

Cooks   Lane

Mursley

Church   Lane   Street

PO   Cemetery

D F

Ma

†

B4032

Richmond Lodge

Merrymead

Stewkley

Shorndown Equine Clinic

Lane

B4032

Lower Dean Farm

Cross Bucks Way

Dean   Road

Stewkley Dean

Cross Bucks Way

Dean

Road

Dean

Blackland Farm

A   B   C   D   E

ROAD

ury

1

2

3

75

4

5

6

1 grid square represents 500 metres

F1
1 Bates Gdns
2 Stones Wy

F4
1 Haywood Pk

F **G** **H** 69 **J** **K** Dorcas Farm

I

Lodge
Industrial
Centre

Prospect Cl

Highway

Drayton Parslow

Stokeroad
Farm

2

3

78

Bletchley Road

The
Grange

4

North End

Stockhall
Crescent

HIGH

Cross Bucks Way

5

Cross Bucks Way

Sycamore Close

Stewkley

STREET

IVY Lane

Fishweir

Vicarage
Farm

6

SOULBURY ROAD

St Michaels C of E
Combined School

NORTH

PO

H6
1 Chapel Sq
2 St Michaels Cl

F **G** **H** **J** **K**

Dove Street

Tythe

Folding
Close

Orkney
Close
Walducks
Close

MANOR

HIGH

STREET

Walducks
Farm

South End

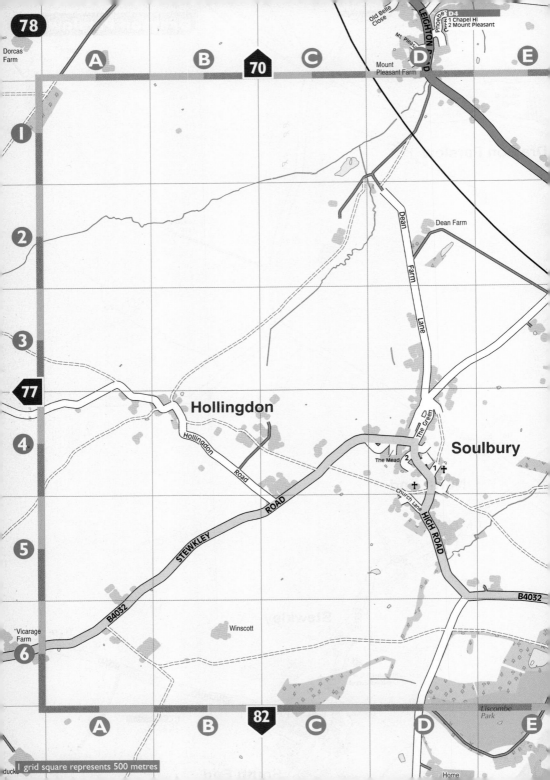

78

Dorcas
Farm

A

B

70

C

Old Belle
Close

Phoebe

LEIGHTON RD

D4
1 Chapel Hi
2 Mount Pleasant

D

E

Mt. Pleas

Mount
Pleasant Farm

I

2

Dean Farm

Dean Farm Lane

3

77

Hollingdon

Hollingdon Road

The Green

4

The Mead

2

Soulbury

Church Lane

1

ROAD

STEWKLEY

HIGH ROAD

5

B4032

B4032

Vicarage
Farm

Winscott

6

A

B

82

C

D

Liscombe
Park

E

ducks

1 grid square represents 500 metres

Home

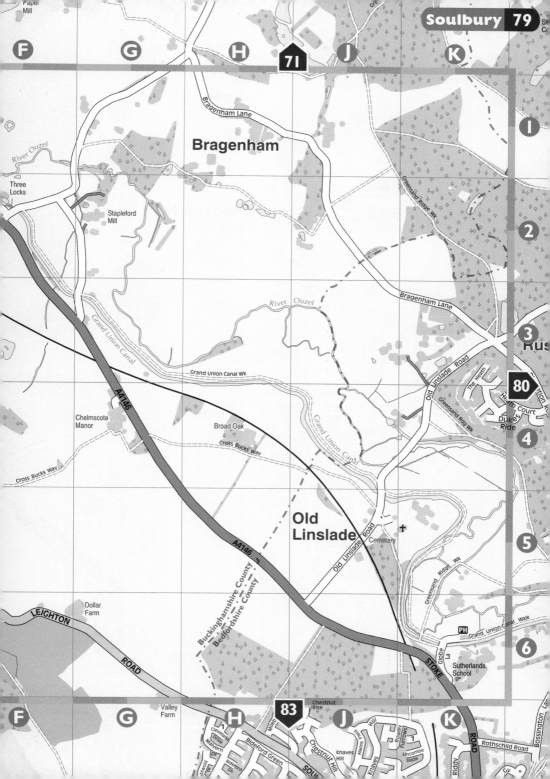

F G H J K

73

Battlesden Park

I

2

3

4

5

6

Eastern Way

A5(T)

Fourne
Hill
Farm

Kingsway
Farm

Mile Tree Road

Miletree
Farm

Lane End
Farm

Hockliffe
Grange

Grange
Farm

Cemetery

Field
Farm

Clipstone

LEIGHTON RC

lip = Brook

F G H J K

85

LEIGHTON ROAD   A4012

Clipstone

F   G   H   **81**   J   K

Clipstone Brook

I

LEIGHTON ROAD A4012

2

Hill Farm

Leighton Road

Eggington

Charity Farm

Orchard Est

High

Church Vw Street

†   †

Mill Road

3

urt
ing Est

Commerce Way Industrial Est

Leighton Road

Concord Way

Mill Road

High Banks

Stanbridge

4

Leighton Road

St Johns (C)

Billington Road

5

Greenacres Farm

6

Billington Road

A4012

Mead Open

A505

F   G   H   J   K

Billington

Akeley	43 K1	Eaglestone	50 A2
Alderton	10 E1	East End	29 J5
Ashton	7 K1	Eggington	85 H2
Aspley Guise	53 F3	Emerson Valley	60 D1
Aspley Heath	52 B6	Far Bletchley	61 F4
Atterbury	38 E3	Fenny Stratford	62 C2
Bancroft	36 C2	Fishermead	3 K7
Bancroft Park	36 C2	Foscote	43 K5
Beachampton	46 C3	Fox Corner	80 C1
Beanhill	49 K4	Fullers Slade	35 H3
Birchmoor Green	65 G3	Furzton	49 G5
Blakelands	26 A4	Gayhurst	15 F1
Bleak Hall	49 J4	Giffard Park	25 H3
Bletchley	61 K1	Gossard's Green	29 K1
Blue Bridge	36 B1	Grafton Regis	11 J1
Bourton	55 H4	Great Brickhill	71 J4
Bow Brickhill	63 H2	Great Holm	48 B1
Bradville	24 D6	Great Horwood	66 C3
Bradwell	36 D3	Great Linford	25 J4
Bradwell Common	36 E4	Green End	71 J3
Bragenham	79 H1	Greenleys	35 J2
Brinklow	51 H1	Greens Norton	4 B1
Broad Green	29 J2	The Green	23 F3
Browns Wood	51 J5	The Green	26 B2
Buckingham	54 D2	Handley	4 B6
Bullington End	13 H5	Haversham	24 A3
Burcott	82 C5	Heath and Reach	80 C2
Caldecote	26 C4	Heathencote	5 K6
Caldecotte	51 F6	Heelands	37 F3
Calverton	35 G6	Hollingdon	78 B4
Castlethorpe	23 G1	Hulcote	5 J1
Central Milton Keynes	2 B4	Hulcote	41 F5
Chackmore	42 E5	Hungate End	12 E1
Chicheley	17 H3	Hurst End	28 C2
Church End	53 H4	Husborne Crawley	53 J4
Clipstone	81 G6	Kents Hill	51 F1
Coffee Hall	49 J3	Kingston	39 H5
The Common	66 C1	Lathbury	16 C4
Conniburrow	2 C1	Leckhampstead	44 C2
Cosgrove	22 E4	Leedon	84 E2
Cranfield	29 J4	Leighton Buzzard	84 C1
Cross End	52 A2	Lillingstone Dayrell	31 H3
Crowhill	48 C2	Lillingstone Lovell	31 J1
Dadford	30 A6	Linslade	83 J2
Deanshanger	33 J3	Little Brickhill	63 J6
Downhead Park	37 K1	Little Horwood	67 G3
Down's Barn	37 K2	Little Linford	15 G6
Drayton Parslow	77 F1	Loughton	48 E1
Duck End	75 G3	Lower End	40 C6
Lower End	56 E2	Shipton	
Lower Weald	35 F5	Shutlanger	
Maids' Moreton	43 J5	Simpson	
Middle Weald	35 F6	Singleborough	
Milton Keynes	49 F2	Soulbury	
Milton Keynes Village	39 G3	Springfield	
Monkston	38 E6	Stanbridge	
Monkston Park	38 D6	Stantonbury	
Moulsoe	27 J5	Stewkley	
Mount Pleasant	54 E4	Stewkley Dean	
Mursley	76 A2	Stoke Bruerne	
Nash	58 D2	Stoke Hammond	
Nearton End	75 J5	Stonebridge	
Neath Hill	37 H1	Stony Stratford	
Netherfield	50 A3	Swanbourne	
New Bradwell	24 C5	Tathall End	
Newlands	38 B3	Tattenhoe	
Newport Pagnell	16 B6	Tew's End	
Newton Longville	69 G2	Thornborough	
North End	77 G4	Thornton	
Northfield	38 E2	Tickford End	
Oakgrove	38 C5	Tongwell	
Oldbrook	49 G1	Towcester	
Old Farm Park	51 K4	Two Mile Ash	
Old Linslade	79 J5	Upper Weald	
Old Stratford	22 B6	Walnut Tree	
Old Wolverton	23 H6	Walton	
Passenham	34 C4	Water Eaton	
Paulerspury	10 A4	Wavendon	
Pennyland	25 K6	Wavendon Gate	
Pineham	26 D6	Westcroft	
Pinfoldpond	64 E5	Whaddon	
Plumpton End	10 B4	Wharley End	
Potsgrove	73 G5	Whittlebury	
Potterspury	21 J3	Wicken	
Pury End	9 J3	Willen	
Puxley	21 J6	Willen Park	
Radclive	54 C2	Winslow	
Rocksley	36 D5	Woburn	
Rushmere	80 A3	Woburn Sands	
Salden	68 B5	Wolverton	
Salford	40 D4	Wolverton Mill	
Sheeplane	72 E3	Wood Burcote	
Shenley Brook End	48 C6	Wood End	
Shenley Church End	48 C3	Wood End	
Shenley Lodge	48 E4	Woolstone	
Shenley Wood	48 C5	Woughton on the Green	
Sherington	17 F1	Wymbush	
Sherington Bridge	16 D4	Yardley Gobion	

USING THE STREET INDEX

Street names are listed alphabetically. Each street name is followed by its postal town or area locality, the Postcode District, the page number, and the reference to the square in which the name is found.

Example: **Abbey Rd** *EAG/OLD/WT* MK6 ....**50** D4 🔲

Some entries are followed by a number in a blue box. This number indicates the location of the street within the referenced grid square. The full street name is listed at the side of the map page.

GENERAL ABBREVIATIONS

ACC	ACCESS	COMM	COMMISSION	F/O	FLYOVER	HTS	H
ALY	ALLEY	CON	CONVENT	FC	FOOTBALL CLUB	HVN	
AP	APPROACH	COT	COTTAGE	FK	FORK	HWY	HI
AR	ARCADE	COTS	COTTAGES	FLD	FIELD	IMP	IM
ASS	ASSOCIATION	CP	CAPE	FLDS	FIELDS	IN	
AV	AVENUE	CPS	COPSE	FLS	FALLS	IND EST	INDUSTRIAL
BCH	BEACH	CR	CREEK	FLS	FLATS	INF	INF
BLDS	BUILDINGS	CREM	CREMATORIUM	FM	FARM	INFO	INFORM
BND	BEND	CRS	CRESCENT	FT	FORT	INT	INTERC
BNK	BANK	CSWY	CAUSEWAY	FWY	FREEWAY	IS	
BR	BRIDGE	CT	COURT	FY	FERRY	JCT	JU
BRK	BROOK	CTRL	CENTRAL	GA	GATE	JTY	
BTM	BOTTOM	CTS	COURTS	GAL	GALLERY	KG	
BUS	BUSINESS	CTYD	COURTYARD	GDN	GARDEN	KNL	
BVD	BOULEVARD	CUTT	CUTTINGS	GDNS	GARDENS	L	
BY	BYPASS	CV	COVE	GLD	GLADE	LA	
CATH	CATHEDRAL	CYN	CANYON	GLN	GLEN	LDG	
CEM	CEMETERY	DEPT	DEPARTMENT	GN	GREEN	LGT	
CEN	CENTRE	DL	DALE	GND	GROUND	LK	
CFT	CROFT	DM	DAM	GRA	GRANGE	LKS	
CH	CHURCH	DR	DRIVE	GRG	GARAGE	LNDG	L
CHA	CHASE	DRO	DROVE	GT	GREAT	LTL	
CHYD	CHURCHYARD	DRY	DRIVEWAY	GTWY	GATEWAY	LWR	
CIR	CIRCLE	DWGS	DWELLINGS	GV	GROVE	MAG	MAGI
CIRC	CIRCUS	E	EAST	HGR	HIGHER	MAN	MAN
CL	CLOSE	EMB	EMBANKMENT	HL	HILL	MD	
CLFS	CLIFFS	EMBY	EMBASSY	HLS	HILLS	MDW	ME
CMP	CAMP	ESP	ESPLANADE	HO	HOUSE	MEM	MEM
CNR	CORNER	EST	ESTATE	HOL	HOLLOW	MKT	M
CO	COUNTY	EX	EXCHANGE	HOSP	HOSPITAL	MKTS	MA
COLL	COLLEGE	EXPY	EXPRESSWAY	HRB	HARBOUR	ML	
COM	COMMON	EXT	EXTENSION	HTH	HEATH	ML	

...MANOR
...MEWS
...MISSION
...MOUNT
...MOUNTAIN
...MOUNTAINS
...MUSEUM
...MOTORWAY
...NORTH
...NORTH EAST
...NORTH WEST
...OVERPASS
...OFFICE
...ORCHARD
...OVAL
...PALACE
...PASSAGE
...PAVILION
...PARADE
...PUBLIC HOUSE
...PARK
...PARKWAY
...PLACE
...PLAIN

PLNS.................PLAINS
PLZ...................PLAZA
POL............POLICE STATION
PR...................PRINCE
PREC.............PRECINCT
PREP...........PREPARATORY
PRIM.............PRIMARY
PROM.........PROMENADE
PRS...........PRINCESS
PT...................PORT
PT...................POINT
PTH.................PATH
PZ.................PIAZZA
QD..............QUADRANT
QU................QUEEN
QY.................QUAY
R....................RIVER
RBT...........ROUNDABOUT
RD...................ROAD
RDG...............RIDGE
REP...........REPUBLIC
RES...........RESERVOIR
RFC......RUGBY FOOTBALL CLUB
RI....................RISE

RP...................RAMP
RW...................ROW
S....................SOUTH
SCH.................SCHOOL
SE..............SOUTH EAST
SER...........SERVICE AREA
SH..................SHORE
SHOP...........SHOPPING
SKWY...........SKYWAY
SMT.............SUMMIT
SOC.............SOCIETY
SP...................SPUR
SPR...........SPRING
SQ.................SQUARE
ST.................STREET
STN...........STATION
STR...........STREAM
STRD...........STRAND
SW..........SOUTH WEST
TDG...........TRADING
TER...........TERRACE
THWY.........THROUGHWAY
TNL.............TUNNEL
TOLL...........TOLLWAY

TPK.............TURNPIKE
TR.................TRACK
TRL.............TRAIL
TWR.............TOWER
U/P...........UNDERPASS
UNI...........UNIVERSITY
UPR.............UPPER
V....................VALE
VA.................VALLEY
VIAD.............VIADUCT
VIL.................VILLA
VIS.............VISTA
VLG.............VILLAGE
VLS.............VILLAS
VW.................VIEW
W....................WEST
WD.................WOOD
WHF.............WHARF
WK.................WALK
WKS.............WALKS
WLS.............WELLS
WY.................WAY
YD.................YARD
YHA.........YOUTH HOSTEL

STCODE TOWNS AND AREA ABBREVIATIONS

...Bradwell
...Brackley
...Bletchley
IN........Buckingham/Winslow
........Central Milton Keynes
H/TMA....Crownhill/Great Holm/
Two Mile Ash

DBGH..................Denbigh
EAG/OLD/WTN.....Eaglestone/Oldbrook/
Woughton
EMV/FZ.....Emerson Valley/Furzton
GTLIN.............Great Linford
LBUZ.............Leighton Buzzard
MKV.........Milton Keynes Village

NPAG.............Newport Pagnell
RBEDW.......Rural Bedford west
RMKN....Rural Milton Keynes north
RMKS/WB.........Rural Milton
Keynes south/Woburn
RNHPTN.......Rural Northampton
SHEN.............Shenley

STSTR.........Stoney Stratford
TOW.............Towcester
WEAT.........Water Eaton
WLLN.............Willen
WOLV.............Wolverton
WTR/OFPK.......Walnut Tree/
Old Park Farm

dex - streets

Abb - Bel

A

Rd BDWL MK13 .... 36 D3
OLD/WT MK6 .... 50 D4 ◘
Wk LBUZ LU7 .... 80 B3
Wy BDWL MK13 .... 36 E1
Cl BDWL MK13 .... 36 E1 ◘
Field EAG/OLD/WT MK6 ..... 50 A1
en Cl BTCHLY MK3 .... 61 J1 ◘
m Cl WLLN MK15 .... 38 B1 ◘
Cl LBUZ LU7 .... 84 E3
an Cl BUCK/WIN MK18 ..... 55 J3 ◘
Wy TOW NN12 .... 8 A6
Bottom LBUZ LU7 .... 80 B6
Cl BUCK/WIN MK18 ..... 55 F2
Ct EAG/OLD/WT MK6 ..... 50 B1
I Av LBUZ LU7 .... 84 E4
on Rd BUCK/WIN MK18 ..... 55 G2
St CMK MK9 .... 3 H1
Ct BTCHLY MK3 .... 61 G2
Cl RMKS/WB MK17 .... 61 F6
n Cl WOLV MK12 .... 35 J2 ◘
Dr WLLN MK15 .... 55 H3
Rd LBUZ LU7 .... 84 C3
Wy WEAT MK2 .... 62 B3
I CMK MK9 .... 3 J3
Ct CNH/GTH/TM MK8 ..... 48 C1
m EAG/OLD/WT MK6 ..... 50 C4 ◘
BDWL MK13 .... 37 F2 ◘
ead WOLV MK12 .... 36 A3
Dr WLLN MK15 .... 26 C6
ks Cl SHEN MK5 .... 48 C3
ra Dr NPAG MK16 .... 26 B3
Pl WOLV MK12 .... 36 A3
t WLLN MK15 .... 38 B6
s Vw SHEN MK5 .... 48 E1
Rd LBUZ LU7 .... 84 D1
r BDWL MK13 .... 36 C4
e Crs BDWL MK13 .... 36 D1
s EMV/FZ MK4 .... 60 C1
I GTLIN MK14 .... 25 J5
ld LBUZ LU7 .... 83 J1
ate NPAG MK16 .... 39 G3 ◘
ge Gv EAG/OLD/WT MK6 ... 38 A6
e Ct WLLN MK15 .... 38 B5 ◘
La CMK MK9 .... 3 J3
BDWL MK13 .... 36 D1
rth MKV MK10 .... 39 F6 ◘
I STSTR MK11 .... 35 F2
n Ga EMV/FZ MK4 .... 60 D4
es Cft GTLIN MK14 .... 25 J5 ◘
WLLN MK15 .... 25 K6
t WTR/OFPK MK7 .... 51 F4 ◘
I BUCK/WIN MK18 .... 74 A3 ◘
y Ct CNH/GTH/TM MK8 .... 48 C1 ◘
m Cl SHEN MK5 .... 48 E4
r BTCHLY MK3 .... 61 J1
v GTLIN MK14 .... 25 C4
y Rd NPAG MK16 .... 26 A2

Anson Rd WOLV MK12 .... 35 K1
Appenine Wy LBUZ LU7 .... 84 D1
Appleacres RMKS/WB MK17 ..... 70 C5
Appleby Heath WEAT MK2 .... 62 C4
Applecroft RMKS/WB MK17 ..... 69 G1
Appleton Ms EMV/FZ MK4 ..... 48 E6 ◘
Appleyard Pl EAG/OLD/WT MK6 ... 2 E7
The Approach CNH/GTH/TM MK8... 36 A4
Aquila Rd LBUZ LU7 .... 84 E1
Arbroath Cl BTCHLY MK3 .... 49 H6 ◘
Arbrook Av BDWL MK13 .... 2 C3
Archers Wls BTCHLY MK3 .... 62 A1 ◘
Ardwell La WOLV MK12 .... 35 J2
Aries Ct LBUZ LU7 .... 84 D1
Arlington Ct EMV/FZ MK4 .... 49 H6
Arlott Crs EAG/OLD/WT MK6 ..... 49 J1
Armourer Dr GTLIN MK14 .... 37 J1
Armstrong Cl CNH/GTH/TM MK8... 48 B3
Arncliffe Dr BDWL MK13 .... 36 E3 ◘
BDWL MK13 .... 37 F2 ◘
Arne La WTR/OFPK MK7 .... 51 J4
Arrow Pl WEAT MK2 .... 70 C1
Arundel Gv BTCHLY MK3 .... 61 H3
Ascot Dr LBUZ LU7 .... 83 H5
Ascot Ms LBUZ LU7 .... 83 J3 ◘
Ascot Pl BTCHLY MK3 .... 61 G4 ◘
Ashburnham Cl BTCHLY MK3 ..... 61 G2 ◘
Ashburn Ham Cl EMV/FZ MK4 ... 61 G2 ◘
Ashburnham Crs LBUZ LU7 ..... 83 K3
Ashby EAG/OLD/WT MK6 .... 49 K1 ◘
Ashdown Cl GTLIN MK14 .... 25 K5 ◘
Ashfield GTLIN MK14 .... 25 G5
Ashfield Gv WEAT MK2 .... 62 B4
Ash Gv DBGH MK1 .... 50 C6
LBUZ LU7 .... 84 B1
Ash Hill Rd NPAG MK16 .... 26 A1
Ashlong Cl LBUZ LU7 .... 84 D2 ◘
Ashpole Furlong SHEN MK5 ..... 48 E2
Ashridge Cl BTCHLY MK3 .... 61 G4
Ashton Rd TOW NN12 .... 7 H1
Ashwell St LBUZ LU7 .... 84 B1
Ashwood BDWL MK13 .... 24 D6
Asplands Cl RMKS/WB MK17 ..... 52 C5
Aspley Hl RMKS/WB MK17 .... 52 D5
Aspley La RMKS/WB MK17 .... 64 E2
Astlethorpe CNH/GTH/TM MK8 ... 36 C5
Aston Cl SHEN MK5 .... 48 E4
Atherstone Ct CNH/GTH/TM MK8.. 35 K5
Atkins Cl BDWL MK13 .... 36 E4
Atterbrook BDWL MK13 .... 36 D3 ◘
Atterbury Av LBUZ LU7 .... 84 C1
Attingham Hl EMV/FZ MK4 ..... 48 C1 ◘
Atwell Cl CNH/GTH/TM MK8..... 48 B2
Auckland Pk DBGH MK1 .... 50 C6
Auden Cl NPAG MK16 .... 15 K6 ◘
Audley Md BDWL MK13 .... 36 D4
Augustus Rd STSTR MK11......... 34 E3
Austins Pl TOW NN12 .... 18 B1
Austwick La EMV/FZ MK4......... 60 E1
Avebury Bvd CMK MK9 .... 3 K2
Avenue Rd BUCK/WIN MK18 ..... 43 H6

BUCK/WIN MK18 .... 74 A3
Avington Cl CNH/GTH/TM MK8 ... 48 B1
Avon Cl NPAG MK16 .... 26 C2
Avon Gv BTCHLY MK3 .... 61 H3
Aylesbury St WEAT MK2 .... 62 D3
WOLV MK12 .... 35 K1
Aylesbury St West WOLV MK12 ... 35 J1
Aynho Ct CNH/GTH/TM MK8 ..... 48 C1 ◘
Ayr Wy BTCHLY MK3 .... 61 H1

B

Baccara Gv WEAT MK2 .... 62 B4
Back St BUCK/WIN MK18 .... 57 F3
Baden Powell Crs TOW NN12 ..... 5 F5 ◘
Badgemore Ct
CNH/GTH/TM MK8 .... 35 K5
Badgers Oak WTR/OFPK MK7 ..... 51 G2
Badgers Wy BUCK/WIN MK18 ..... 55 H4
Badminton Vw
CNH/GTH/TM MK8 .... 36 D6 ◘
Baily Ct SHEN MK5 .... 48 D4 ◘
Bairstow Rd TOW NN12 .... 5 F4
Bakers La TOW NN12 .... 7 F1
Baker St LBUZ LU7 .... 84 B2
Bakers Wood Cl LBUZ LU7 .... 80 B1
Bakery Cl RBEDW MK43 .... 29 J4 ◘
Bala Wy WEAT MK2 .... 62 B5
Balfe Ms WTR/OFPK MK7 .... 51 J5
Ball Moor BUCK/WIN MK18 ..... 55 H6
Balmer Br BUCK/WIN MK18 ..... 55 H6
Balmer Cut BUCK/WIN MK18 ..... 55 G5
Balmerino Cl MKV MK10 .... 39 G5
Balmoral Cl TOW NN12 .... 4 E4
Balsam Cl WTR/OFPK MK7 .... 51 G3
Bampton Cl EMV/FZ MK4 .... 61 H1
Banktop Pl EMV/FZ MK4 .... 49 F6
Bantock Cl WTR/OFPK MK7 ..... 51 H4
Barbers Ms GTLIN MK14 .... 37 J1 ◘
Barbury Ct GTLIN MK14............. 25 K5
Bardsey Ct MKV MK10............. 39 F5
Barford STSTR MK11 .... 35 G3
Barkestone Cl EMV/FZ MK4 ..... 61 H1
Barleycorn Cl LBUZ LU7 .... 84 E2 ◘
Barleycroft EMV/FZ MK4 .... 48 D6
Barnabas Rd LBUZ LU7 .... 83 J3 ◘
Barnes Pl EAG/OLD/WT MK6 ..... 49 H1 ◘
Barnfield Dr EAG/OLD/WT MK6 ... 50 B3
Barnsbury Gdns NPAG MK16 ..... 26 B2
Barnsdale Dr EMV/FZ MK4......... 60 C1
Barons Cl WEAT MK2 .... 62 B3
Barrett Pl SHEN MK5 .... 48 C3
Barry Av BDWL MK13 .... 25 F6
Bartholomew Cl WTR/OFPK MK7 .. 51 F4
Bartlett Pl BUCK/WIN MK18 ..... 55 H2
Barton Rd WEAT MK2 .... 62 B5
Bascote EAG/OLD/WT MK6......... 50 C4
Basildon Ct CNH/GTH/TM MK8 .. 48 C1 ◘

LBUZ LU7 .... 84 A1 ◘
Baskerfield Gv EAG/⊖LD/WT MK6.. 50 B1
Bassett Ct NPAG MK16 .... 26 B1 ◘
Bassett Rd LBUZ LU7 .... 84 A2
Bates Cl WLLN MK15 .... 26 C6
Bates Gdns RMKS/WB MK17 ..... 77 F1 ◘
Bath La BUCK/WIN MK18 .... 55 F3
Battlesden Av RMKS/WB MK17 ... 73 J6
Baxter Cl CNH/GTH/TM MK8 ..... 48 B2
Bayard Av GTLIN MK14 .... 37 J2 ◘
Baynham Md WTR/OFPK MK7 ... 51 G1 ◘
Bay Tree Cl RMKS/WB MK17 ..... 69 G1
Beacon Ct EMV/FZ MK4 .... 61 G1
Beaconsfield Pl NPAG MK16 ..... 26 B1 ◘
Beadlemead EAG/OLD/WT MK6... 50 B3
Beales La WTR/OFPK MK7 .... 51 F4
Beamish Wy BUCK/WIN MK18 ... 74 C2
Beanfare EAG/OLD/WT MK6......... 50 A5
Beauchamp Cl GTLIN MK14 ..... 25 H6
Beaudesert LBUZ LU7 .... 84 B2
Beaufort Dr WLLN MK15............. 26 B6
Beaumaris Gv SHEN MK5 .... 48 D3
Beaverbook Ct BTCHLY MK3 ..... 61 J2
Beaver Cl BUCK/WIN MK18 ..... 55 H4 ◘
Beckinsale Gv
CNH/GTH/TM MK8 .... 48 B2 ◘
Bec La WLLN MK15 .... 26 A6
Bedford Rd NPAG MK16 .... 17 F2
RBEDW MK43 .... 29 K3
RBEDW MK43 .... 53 H4
Bedford St LBUZ LU7 .... 84 B2
RMKS/WB MK17 .... 65 G4
WEAT MK2 .... 62 B3
WOLV MK12 .... 36 A1
Bedgebury Pl WTR/OFPK MK7... 51 F1
Bedlam La NPAG MK16 .... 17 H2
The Beechams RMKS/WB MK17 ... 76 A1
Beech Cl BUCK/WIN MK18 .... 55 G1
TOW NN12 .... 5 F5
Beechcroft Rd BTCHLY MK3 ..... 61 H5
The Beeches RMKN MK19............. 33 K4
Beech Fern WTR/OFPK MK7 ..... 51 F4 ◘
Beech Gv LBUZ LU7 .... 83 G2
Beech House Dr TOW NN12 ..... 21 K2
Beech Rd NPAG MK16 .... 26 A2
Beethoven Cl WTR/OFPK MK7 ... 51 K5
Beeward Cl WOLV MK12 .... 35 H2
Bekonscot Ct GTLIN MK14 .... 25 J4
Bell Aly BUCK/WIN MK18 .... 74 A4
Bell Cl RMKS/WB MK17 .... 76 E2
Belle Baulk TOW NN12 .... 4 D3
Bellini Cl WTR/OFPK MK7 .... 51 J4
Bellis Gv EAG/OLD/WT MK6 ..... 50 B1
Bells Meadow WLLN MK15 ..... 26 A6 ◘
Bellway RMKS/WB MK17 .... 52 A3
Bellwether STSTR MK11 .... 35 H3
Belmont Ct CNH/GTH/TM MK8 .. 35 K5 ◘
Belsize Av EAG/OLD/WT MK6 ..... 38 A6
Belvedere GTLIN MK14 .... 3 G1
Belvedere La WEAT MK2 .... 62 E3
Belvoir Av EMV/FZ MK4 .... 61 F2

Benbow Ct *SHEN* MK5 .... 48 D2 ▫
Bengal La *TOW* NN12 .... 4 A2
Bengal Vw *TOW* NN12 .... 4 B2
Bennett Cl *STSTR* MK11 .... 35 F3
Bens Cl *RMKN* MK19 .... 13 G6
Bentall Cl *WLLN* MK15 .... 26 B6 ▫
Benwell Cl *BDWL* MK13 .... 36 C2 ▫
Berberis Cl *WTR/OFPK* MK7 ...... 51 F4
Bercham *CNH/GTH/TM* MK8 ..... 36 B5
Beretun *CNH/GTH/TM* MK8 .... 36 B6
Berevilles La *MKV* MK10 .... 38 D5
Bergamot Gdns *WTR/OFPK* MK7 .. 51 G4
Berling Rd *CNH/GTH/TM* MK8 .... 36 C5
Bernay Gdns *WLLN* MK15 .... 26 A6
Bernstein Cl *WTR/OFPK* MK7 ..... 51 H5
Berry La *RMKS/WB* MK17 .... 53 F3
Berrystead *WTR/OFPK* MK7 ..... 51 G6 ▫
Berry Wy *RMKS/WB* MK17 .... 69 F1
Berwald Cl *WTR/OFPK* MK7 .... 51 J5
Berwick Dr *BTCHLY* MK3 .... 61 J1
Bessemer Ct *GTLIN* MK14 .... 25 K4
Bettina Gv *WEAT* MK2 .... 62 B4
Betty's Cl *RMKS/WB* MK17 .... 69 F1
Beverley Pl *EAG/OLD/WT* MK6 ... 38 A5
Bewdley Dr *LBUZ* LU7 .... 83 H2
Bickerstaffes Rd *TOW* NN12 ...... 5 F4
Bickleigh Crs *EMV/FZ* MK4 .... 49 F6
Bideford Gn *LBUZ* LU7 .... 83 H1
Bignell Cft *SHEN* MK5 .... 36 E6
Bilbrook La *EMV/FZ* MK4 .... 49 F5
Billington Ct *LBUZ* LU7 .... 84 C3 ▫
Billington Rd *LBUZ* LU7 .... 84 B3
     LBUZ LU7 .... 85 J5
Billingwell Pl *EAG/OLD/WT* MK6 .. 38 A4
Bilton Rd *DBGH* MK1 .... 62 C2
Bingham Ct *EMV/FZ* MK4 .... 61 F2
Birchen Lee *EMV/FZ* MK4 .... 61 F1 ▫
Birchfield Gv *WEAT* MK2 .... 62 B4
Birdlip La *WTR/OFPK* MK7 .... 51 G2
Bird's Hl *LBUZ* LU7 .... 80 B2
Birkdale Cl *BTCHLY* MK3 .... 61 G4
Bishopstone Rd *BDWL* MK13 ...... 2 C2
Blackberry Ct *WTR/OFPK* MK7 ... 51 G3 ▫
Blackdown *STSTR* MK11 .... 35 G3
Blackham Ct
     EAG/OLD/WT MK6 .... 49 H2 ▫
Blackheath Crs *BDWL* MK13 ...... 2 C2
Blackhill Dr *WOLV* MK12 .... 35 H1
Blackmoor Ga *EMV/FZ* MK4 ...... 61 H1
Blackthorn Gv *RMKS/WB* MK17 .. 52 B5
Blackwell Cl *TOW* NN12 .... 5 G5
Blackwell End *TOW* NN12 .... 21 H2
Blackwell Pl *SHEN* MK5 .... 48 D5
Blackwood Crs *BDWL* MK13 .... 36 B1
Blairmont St *CMK* MK9 .... 37 J3
Blakedown Rd *LBUZ* LU7 .... 83 H3
Blakeney Ct *EMV/FZ* MK4 .... 60 E3
Blatherwick Ct *SHEN* MK5 .... 48 C2 ▫
Blaydon Cl *BTCHLY* MK3 .... 61 G5
Bleasdale *BDWL* MK13 .... 37 F2 ▫
Blenheim Av *STSTR* MK11 .... 35 F3
Bletcham Wy *DBGH* MK1 .... 62 D1
     EAG/OLD/WT MK6 .... 50 E6
     WTR/OFPK MK7 .... 51 H4
Bletchley Rd *LBUZ* LU7 .... 77 G4
     RMKS/WB MK17 .... 69 G3
     SHEN MK5 .... 48 E5
Bliss Av *RBEDW* MK43 .... 29 K3
Bliss Ct *WTR/OFPK* MK7 .... 51 H5
Blisworth *EAG/OLD/WT* MK6 ..... 50 C4
Bloomsbury Cl
     RMKS/WB MK17 .... 65 G5 ▫
Bluebell Ct *WTR/OFPK* MK7 ...... 51 G3
Blundells Rd *BDWL* MK13 .... 36 E1
Blythe Cl *NPAG* MK16 .... 26 C2 ▫
Bodenham Cl *BUCK/WIN* MK18 .. 55 J3
Bodiam Cl *SHEN* MK5 .... 48 D4
Bodle Cl *WLLN* MK15 .... 25 K6
Bodnant Ct *EMV/FZ* MK4 .... 60 C1 ▫
Bolan Ct *CNH/GTH/TM* MK8 ..... 48 B3
Bolton Cl *BTCHLY* MK3 .... 61 K1
Bond Av *DBGH* MK1 .... 50 C6
Bonnards Rd *RMKS/WB* MK17 ... 69 G1
Booker Av *BDWL* MK13 .... 2 C2
Bossard Ct *LBUZ* LU7 .... 84 B2
Bossiney Pl *EAG/OLD/WT* MK6 ... 3 H6
Bossington La *LBUZ* LU7 .... 83 K2
Boswell Ct *BUCK/WIN* MK18 ...... 55 H2
Boswell La *RMKN* MK19 .... 33 J3
Bosworth Cl *BTCHLY* MK3 .... 61 H1 ▫
Bottesford Cl *EMV/FZ* MK4 .... 61 G2 ▫
Boulters Lock *GTLIN* MK14 .... 25 J3
Boundary Crs *STSTR* MK11 .... 35 F1
The Boundary *EAG/OLD/WT* MK6 .. 49 J1
Bounty St *BDWL* MK13 .... 24 C6
Bourne End Rd *RBEDW* MK43 .... 29 J1
Bourton Low *WTR/OFPK* MK7 .... 51 G4
Bourton Rd *BUCK/WIN* MK18 ..... 55 K3

Bourtonville *BUCK/WIN* MK18 ... 55 G4
Bow Brickhill Rd *RMKS/WB* MK17.. 52 A6
Bowen Cl *WTR/OFPK* MK7 .... 51 H4 ▫
Bowes Cl *NPAG* MK16 .... 26 B2 ▫
Bowland Dr *EMV/FZ* MK4 .... 60 E2
Bowling Green Rd *RBEDW* MK43 .. 29 K4
Bowling Leys *MKV* MK10 .... 39 F5
Bowood Ct *CNH/GTH/TM* MK8 .. 36 C6 ▫
Bowyers Ms *GTLIN* MK14 .... 37 J1
Boxberry Gdns *WTR/OFPK* MK7 .. 51 F3
Boyce Crs *WTR/OFPK* MK7 .... 51 J4
Boycott Av *EAG/OLD/WT* MK6 ... 3 F7
Bozenham Mill La *TOW* NN12 .... 7 J6
Brabham Cl *TOW* NN12 .... 18 A1 ▫
Brackley Rd *TOW* NN12 .... 4 E3
Bradbourne Dr *WTR/OFPK* MK7 .. 51 H5
Bradbury Cl *BDWL* MK13 .... 36 D4
Bradden Wy *TOW* NN12 .... 4 A1
Bradfield Av *BUCK/WIN* MK18 .... 55 G1
Bradvue Crs *BDWL* MK13 .... 36 D1
Bradwell Common Bvd
     BDWL MK13 .... 2 B3
Bradwell Rd *BDWL* MK13 .... 24 D6
     CNH/GTH/TM MK8 .... 36 D5
     SHEN MK5 .... 48 D2
Braford Gdns *SHEN* MK5 .... 48 E5
Bragenham La *RMKS/WB* MK17 .. 79 H1
Bragenham Side
     RMKS/WB MK17 .... 70 D6
Brahms Cl *WTR/OFPK* MK7 .... 51 H4
Bramber Cl *BTCHLY* MK3 .... 61 H4
Bramble Av *GTLIN* MK14 .... 37 H3
Bramble Cl *LBUZ* LU7 .... 84 D2 ▫
Bramble Rd *TOW* NN12 .... 4 E5
Bramley Rd *DBGH* MK1 .... 62 B1
Bransgill Ct *BDWL* MK13 .... 36 E3 ▫
Bransworth Av *MKV* MK10 .... 51 H1
Brantham Cl *WTR/OFPK* MK7 .... 51 F6 ▫
Braunston *EAG/OLD/WT* MK6 .... 50 C3
Braybrooke Dr *EMV/FZ* MK4 ..... 49 H6
Brayton Ct *SHEN* MK5 .... 49 F3
Breamore Ct *CNH/GTH/TM* MK8 .. 48 C1
Brearley Av *EAG/OLD/WT* MK6 ... 49 H2
Bremen Gv *SHEN* MK5 .... 48 D5
Brendon Ct *EMV/FZ* MK4 .... 49 G6
Brent *EAG/OLD/WT* MK6 .... 50 C4
Bretby Cha *EMV/FZ* MK4 .... 60 C1
Breton *STSTR* MK11 .... 35 F1
Briar Hl *WOLV* MK12 .... 36 A2
Briary Cl *TOW* NN12 .... 4 E5 ▫
Briary Vw *RMKS/WB* MK17 .... 59 J3
Brices Meadow *SHEN* MK5 .... 48 D6 ▫
Brick Cl *STSTR* MK11 .... 35 K5
Brickhill Rd *LBUZ* LU7 .... 72 B6
Brickhill St *GTLIN* MK14 .... 25 K5
     MKV MK10 .... 38 E6
     WLLN MK15 .... 26 A5
     WTR/OFPK MK7 .... 50 E1
Brick Kiln Cl *TOW* NN12 .... 5 F5
Bridgeford Ct *EAG/OLD/WT* MK6 .. 49 H1
Bridge Rd *RMKN* MK19 .... 23 F3
Bridge St *BDWL* MK13 .... 24 C6
     BUCK/WIN MK18 .... 55 G3
     RMKN MK18 .... 87 F4
     LBUZ LU7 .... 84 D2 ▫
Bridgeturn Av *WOLV* MK12 .... 24 A5
Bridgeway *BDWL* MK13 .... 24 D6
Bridle Cl *BDWL* MK13 .... 36 E1 ▫
Bridlington Crs *WTR/OFPK* MK7 .. 38 E6
Brill Pl *BDWL* MK13 .... 36 E4
Brindlebrook *CNH/GTH/TM* MK8.. 36 B6
Bristle Hl *BUCK/WIN* MK18 .... 55 F3 ▫
Bristow Cl *WEAT* MK2 .... 62 D2
Britten Gv *WTR/OFPK* MK7 ...... 51 J4
Brittons La *RMKS/WB* MK17 ..... 40 D4
Broad Arrow Cl *GTLIN* MK14 ..... 25 H6 ▫
Broad Dean *EAG/OLD/WT* MK6 .. 49 K1 ▫
Broadlands *EAG/OLD/WT* MK6.... 50 A3
Broad Piece *WLLN* MK15 .... 25 K6
Broad St *NPAG* MK16 .... 26 B2
Broadwater *EAG/OLD/WT* MK6 .. 50 C4 ▫
Broadwater La *TOW* NN12 .... 4 D4 ▫
Broadway Av *GTLIN* MK14 .... 25 K5
Brockhampton *WLLN* MK15 ...... 38 A1 ▫
Brockwell *NPAG* MK16 .... 26 B1 ▫
Bromham Ml *GTLIN* MK14 .... 25 K5
Brooke Cl *BTCHLY* MK3 .... 61 J4
Brookfield La *BUCK/WIN* MK18 .. 55 G4
Brookfield Rd *RMKN* MK19 .... 24 A3
     RMKS/WB MK17 .... 69 G2
Brooklands Av *LBUZ* LU7 .... 84 C3
Brooklands Dr *LBUZ* LU7 .... 84 C3
Brooklands Rd *WEAT* MK2 .... 62 B3
Brook La *TOW* NN12 .... 4 D3 ▫
Brooks Cl *BUCK/WIN* MK18 .... 55 G3
Brookside *BUCK/WIN* MK18 ...... 31 K2
     WOLV MK12 .... 36 A3
Brookside Cl *RMKN* MK19 .... 34 C1

Brookside Wk *LBUZ* LU7 .... 84 D2
Brook St *LBUZ* LU7 .... 84 D2
Brookway *RMKN* MK19 .... 33 J5
Broomfield *WOLV* MK12 .... 36 A3 ▫
Broomhills Rd *LBUZ* LU7 .... 80 B6
Brough Cl *SHEN* MK5 .... 48 D4
Broughton Rd *MKV* MK10 .... 39 F4
     RMKS/WB MK17 .... 40 D4
Brownbaker Ct *GTLIN* MK14 ..... 37 J1 ▫
Browne Willis Cl *WEAT* MK2 ...... 62 C3
Browning Cl *NPAG* MK16 .... 25 K1
Browning Crs *BTCHLY* MK3 .... 61 K4
Brownsfield Rd *TOW* NN12 .... 11 K5
Brownslea *LBUZ* LU7 .... 84 D2 ▫
Browns Wy *RMKS/WB* MK17 ..... 53 F4
Brownswood Dr *TOW* NN12 ...... 21 J2 ▫
Broxbourne Cl *GTLIN* MK14 ...... 25 J3 ▫
Bruckner Gdns
     WTR/OFPK MK7 .... 51 J4 ▫
Brudenell Dr *MKV* MK10 .... 51 H1
Bruleys Ct *EMV/FZ* MK4 .... 49 G6 ▫
Bryony Pl *GTLIN* MK14 .... 37 H2
Buckby *EAG/OLD/WT* MK6 .... 50 C4
Buckfast Av *BTCHLY* MK3 .... 61 K1
Buckingham Ga
     EAG/OLD/WT MK6 .... 38 A6 ▫
Buckingham Rd *BTCHLY* MK3 .... 61 K4
     RMKN MK19 .... 34 A4
Buckingham Sq *CMK* MK9 .... 2 B5 ▫
Buckingham St *WOLV* MK12 ...... 36 A1
Buckingham Wy *TOW* NN12 ...... 4 E4
Buckland Dr *EAG/OLD/WT* MK6.. 50 B3
Buckley Ct *STSTR* MK11 .... 35 G3
Buckman Cl *WOLV* MK12 .... 35 J2 ▫
Buckthorn *WOLV* MK12 .... 36 B2
Budge Rd *TOW* NN12 .... 12 A6
Bullington End Rd *RMKN* MK19 .. 13 H5
Bunkers La *LBUZ* LU7 .... 83 J5
Burano Cl *WTR/OFPK* MK7 .... 51 H3
Burchard Crs *SHEN* MK5 .... 48 D3
Burcote Rd *TOW* NN12 .... 5 G4
Burdeleys La *SHEN* MK5 .... 48 D5
Burdock Cl *NPAG* MK16 .... 25 J1 ▫
Burewelle *CNH/GTH/TM* MK8 .... 36 A6
Burgess Gdns *NPAG* MK16 .... 26 A3
Burghley Ct *CNH/GTH/TM* MK8 .. 48 C1
Burholme *EMV/FZ* MK4 .... 49 F6
Burleigh Piece *BUCK/WIN* MK18 .. 55 H2
Burleys Rd *BUCK/WIN* MK18 ..... 74 A3
Burners La *STSTR* MK11 .... 35 J3
Burners La South *STSTR* MK11 .. 35 J4
Burnet *GTLIN* MK14 .... 25 F6
Burnham Dr *BDWL* MK13 .... 2 B2
Burnmoor Cl *WEAT* MK2 .... 70 C1
Burns Cl *NPAG* MK16 .... 25 K1
Burns Rd *BTCHLY* MK3 .... 61 K4
Burrows Cl *RMKS/WB* MK17 ...... 52 C4
Burtree Cl *WOLV* MK12 .... 36 A2
Bury Av *NPAG* MK16 .... 26 B1
Bury St *NPAG* MK16 .... 26 B1
Busby Cl *BUCK/WIN* MK18 .... 55 J2
Buscot Pl *CNH/GTH/TM* MK8 .... 48 C1
Bushey Bartrams *SHEN* MK5 ..... 48 D6
Bushey Cl *BUCK/WIN* MK18 ...... 55 J2
Bushy Cl *BTCHLY* MK3 .... 49 K6
Bute La *EMV/FZ* MK4 .... 60 C1
Butlers Gv *GTLIN* MK14 .... 25 G5
Butterfield Cl *WLLN* MK15 .... 38 B5
Buttermere Cl *WEAT* MK2 .... 62 C5
Buzzacott La *EMV/FZ* MK4 .... 49 F6
Bycell Rd *BUCK/WIN* MK18 .... 42 E1
Byerly Pl *GTLIN* MK14 .... 37 J2
Byford Wy *BUCK/WIN* MK18 ..... 74 A3
Byrd Crs *WTR/OFPK* MK7 .... 51 J3
Byron Cl *BTCHLY* MK3 .... 61 J4
     TOW NN12 .... 4 E4
Byron Dr *NPAG* MK16 .... 25 K1
Byward Cl *GTLIN* MK14 .... 25 H6 ▫

C

Cadman Sq *SHEN* MK5 .... 49 F4
Caernarvon Cl *TOW* NN12 .... 5 F5
Caernarvon Crs *BTCHLY* MK3 .... 61 G4
Caesars Cl *BDWL* MK13 .... 36 D2
Cairngorm Ga *EAG/OLD/WT* MK6 .. 49 G1
Caithness Ct *BTCHLY* MK3 .... 49 H6
Calamus Ct *WTR/OFPK* MK7 ..... 51 G3 ▫
Caldecote La *NPAG* MK16 .... 26 B1
Caldecote St *NPAG* MK16 .... 26 B1
Caldecotte Lake Dr
     WTR/OFPK MK7 .... 63 F1
Caldecotte La *WTR/OFPK* MK7 .. 51 F6

Calder Gdns *LBUZ* LU7 .... 84 D2
Caldewell *CNH/GTH/TM* MK8 .... 36 B6
Caledonian Rd *BDWL* MK13 ......
Calewen *CNH/GTH/TM* MK8 ...... 36 B6
Calluna Dr *BTCHLY* MK3 ....
Calverleigh Crs *EMV/FZ* MK4 ....
Calvert Cl *TOW* NN12 ....
Calverton La *RMKN* MK19 ....
Calverton Rd *STSTR* MK11 ....
Calvert Rd *TOW* NN12 ....
Calves Cl *SHEN* MK5 ....
Camber Cl *BTCHLY* MK3 ....
Camberton Rd *LBUZ* LU7 ....
Cambridge St *WEAT* MK2 ....
     WOLV MK12 ....
Cambron *CNH/GTH/TM* MK8 .....
Cam Ct *BTCHLY* MK3 ....
Camlet Gv *GTLIN* MK14 ....
Camomile Ct *WTR/OFPK* MK7 ...
Campania Cl *MKV* MK10 ....
Campbell Cl *BUCK/WIN* MK18....
Candlewicks *WTR/OFPK* MK7 ....
Canons Rd *WOLV* MK12 ....
The Canons *NPAG* MK16 ....
Cantell Cl *BUCK/WIN* MK18 ......
Cantle Av *GTLIN* MK14 ....
Capel Cl *BUCK/WIN* MK18 ....
Capel Dr *GTLIN* MK14 ....
Capital Dr *GTLIN* MK14 ....
Cappenham Br *TOW* NN12 ....
Cappenham Ct *TOW* NN12 ....
Capron *EAG/OLD/WT* MK6 ....
Capshill Av *LBUZ* LU7 ....
Caraway Cl *WTR/OFPK* MK7 .....
Cardwell Cl *EMV/FZ* MK4 ....
Carey Rd *TOW* NN12 ....
Careys Rd *TOW* NN12 ....
Carhampton Ct *EMV/FZ* MK4 ....
Carina Dr *LBUZ* LU7 ....
Carisbrooke Ct
     BUCK/WIN MK18 ....
Carleton Ga *WLLN* MK15 ....
Carlina Pl *GTLIN* MK14 ....
Carlton Cl *NPAG* MK16 ....
Carlton Gv *LBUZ* LU7 ....
Carlyle Cl *NPAG* MK16 ....
Carnation Cl *LBUZ* LU7 ....
The Carne *STSTR* MK11 ....
Carnot Cl *SHEN* MK5 ....
Carnoustie Cl *BTCHLY* MK3 ......
Carolus Creek *WLLN* MK15 ....
Carpenter Ct *GTLIN* MK14 ....
Carrick Rd *EAG/OLD/WT* MK6....
Carrington Rd *NPAG* MK16 ....
Carroll Cl *NPAG* MK16 ....
Carron Cl *LBUZ* LU7 ....
Carron Ct *WEAT* MK2 ....
Carteret Cl *WLLN* MK15 ....
Carters Cl *NPAG* MK16 ....
Carters La *STSTR* MK11 ....
Cartmel Cl *BTCHLY* MK3 ....
Cartwright Pl
     EAG/OLD/WT MK6 ....
Carvers Ms *GTLIN* MK14 ....
Cashmere Cl *SHEN* MK5 ....
Casterton Cl *BDWL* MK13 ....
Castle Cl *LBUZ* LU7 ....
Castle Meadow Cl *LBUZ* LU7 ....
Castle Rose *EAG/OLD/WT* MK6 ..
Castlesteads *BDWL* MK13 ....
Castle St *BUCK/WIN* MK18 ....
Castlethorpe Rd *RMKN* MK19 ...
Catchpole Cl *WOLV* MK12 ....
Cathay Cl *BTCHLY* MK3 ....
Catherine Ct
     BUCK/WIN MK18 ....
Cattleford Br *RMKS/WB* MK17...
Cavendish Ct *SHEN* MK5 ....
Cavenham *CNH/GTH/TM* MK8 ...
Cawardon *GTLIN* MK14 ....
Cawkwell Wy *WEAT* MK2 ....
Caxton Rd *WOLV* MK12 ....
Cecily Ct *SHEN* MK5 ....
Cedar Cl *TOW* NN12 ....
Cedars Cl *BUCK/WIN* MK18 ......
Cedars Wy *LBUZ* LU7 ....
     NPAG MK16 ....
Celandine Ct *WTR/OFPK* MK7 ...
Celina Cl *WEAT* MK2 ....
Centauri Cl *LBUZ* LU7 ....
Central Av *RBEDW* MK43 ....
Centurion Ct *STSTR* MK11 ....
Century Av *EAG/OLD/WT* MK6 ...
Cetus Crs *LBUZ* LU7 ....
Chadds La *EAG/OLD/WT* MK6 ...
Chadwick Dr *EAG/OLD/WT* MK6
Chaffron Wy *EAG/OLD/WT* MK6
     EMV/FZ MK4 ....

MK10 .... 38 E5
MK5 .... 49 G3
MK15 .... 38 B6
PI CNH/GTH/TM MK8 .... 48 C1
II Dr SHEN MK5 .... 48 C4
ombe EMV/FZ MK4 .... 61 G1
rs Av RMKN MK19 .... 24 A3
r Ct LBUZ LU7 .... 84 C4
I Rdg SHEN MK5 .... 48 E5
rlains Gdn LBUZ LU7 ... 80 B6
lower EMV/FZ MK4 ...... 49 C6 ⑥
y Cl BDWL MK13 .... 36 D1 ⑥
rs Ct EAG/OLD/WT MK6 .. 50 D4
s Cl BUCK/WIN MK18 .... 55 C4
s CI BUCK/WIN MK18 ..... 55 C4
I Cl RMKS/WB MK17 .... 52 B4
La TOW NN12 .... 5 F3
I LBUZ LU7 .... 78 D4 ⑥
II LBUZ LU7 .... 78 D4 ⑥
a BUCK/WIN MK18 .... 43 K1
WIN MK18 .... 57 F3
/WB MK17 .... 76 E1
N12 .... 7 F1
Sq LBUZ LU7 .... 77 H6 ⑥
st RMKS/WB MK17 .... 52 C5
Gv CNH/GTH/TM MK8 .... 36 B6
n Av GTLIN MK14 .... 37 K2
re CNH/GTH/TM MK8 .... 36 B6
wy NPAG MK16 .... 26 B1 ④
x Ct NPAG MK16 .... 25 J1 ②
I Cl RMKS/WB MK17 .... 75 H4 ②
t Ct SHEN MK5 .... 48 C5
or Rd LBUZ LU7 .... 84 B5
ll Rd NPAG MK16 .... 26 D2 ②
y WTR/OFPK MK7 .... 51 F5
se RMKS/WB MK17 ..... 69 G2 ⑥
rth CNH/GTH/TM MK8 ... 36 C6
Cl NPAG MK16 .... 25 K1
Rt BTCHLY MK3 .... 61 K4
n Crs CNH/GTH/TM MK8 ... 36 C6
Gn LBUZ LU7 .... 83 J3
ham Gdns
y MK3 .... 61 G5 ⑥
k BTCHLY MK3 .... 49 K6
r's End
WIN MK18 .... 74 B3 ⑥
w Dr BTCHLY MK3 .... 61 G5
uers RMKN MK19 .... 13 C6
a EMV/FZ MK4 .... 49 H6
n CNH/GTH/TM MK8 ...... 36 B6
ourt Wy LBUZ LU7 ...... 84 E2
d NPAG MK16 .... 26 A2
EAG/OLD/WT MK6 .... 50 A4
n Av BDWL MK13 .... 2 B2
Gdns GTLIN MK14 .... 25 K5 ②
Wold EAG/OLD/WT MK6 .. 49 J3
l BTCHLY MK3 .... 61 G4 ⑥
ield Crs LBUZ LU7 ...... 82 D6
nolm BDWL MK13 .... 36 C2
Cl RMKS/WB MK17 ..... 69 G3
MK11 .... 34 E2
t Crs WEAT MK2 .... 62 C4
t HI LBUZ LU7 .... 83 J1
t Ri LBUZ LU7 .... 83 J1
t Rd TOW NN12 .... 12 A5
PI TOW NN12 .... 21 K3
de Av WTR/OFPK MK7 ... 39 F6
de Cl BUCK/WIN MK18 ... 55 H1 ⑥
er Gv CNH/GTH/TM MK8 .. 48 A2
Cl LBUZ LU7 .... 83 H1 ⑥
t BUCK/WIN MK18 ...... 55 J2 ⑥
y HI NPAG MK16 .... 16 E3
y Rd NPAG MK16 .... 17 H3
y St NPAG MK16 .... 26 D1
nds Av MKV MK10 .... 39 F6
Ct EMV/FZ MK4 .... 61 F2
y EAG/OLD/WT MK6 .... 2 E7
Z MK4 .... 60 B1
K10 .... 38 E3
MK5 .... 48 C5
Leys WLLN MK15 .... 26 D6 ②
am Ct SHEN MK5 .... 48 C5
Ct BUCK/WIN MK18 ..... 74 A4 ⑥
Gdns LBUZ LU7 .... 80 B4 ⑥
terns LBUZ LU7 .... 84 D3
Cft EMV/FZ MK4 .... 61 F1
ham Dr MKV MK10 .... 39 F6
Field Rd BDWL MK13 .... 24 D6
g V EMV/FZ MK4 .... 61 F1
mpton WLLN MK15 ...... 38 B4 ⑥
Cl EMV/FZ MK4 .... 60 C1
Ct WLLN MK15 .... 26 B5
Cl NPAG MK16 .... 15 K6
Av LBUZ LU7 .... 84 B3
BUCK/WIN MK18 .... 43 J6

RMKN MK19 .... 33 G4
Church End BUCK/WIN MK18 .... 44 C1
NPAG MK16 .... 17 F1
RMKS/WB MK17 .... 51 K2
RMKS/WB MK17 .... 69 G2 ⑥
TOW NN12 .... 21 K2
Church End Rd SHEN MK5 .... 48 D5
Church Green Rd BTCHLY MK3 .... 61 J4
Church HI BUCK/WIN MK18 .... 43 J1
CNH/GTH/TM MKB 36 B5
RMKS/WB MK17 .... 53 F4
TOW NN12 .... 59 J2
Churchill Rd LBUZ LU7 .... 80 C6
Church La BUCK/WIN MK18 .... 31 K2
BUCK/WIN MK18 .... 57 F3
LBUZ LU7 .... 78 D4
NPAG MK16 .... 16 B5
RMKN MK19 .... 33 K3
RMKS/WB MK17 .... 59 J2
RMKS/WB MK17 .... 75 K2
SHEN MK5 .... 48 E1
TOW NN12 .... 7 F1
TOW NN12 .... 10 E1
TOW NN12 .... 21 K2
Church Lees GTLIN MK14 .... 25 G4
Church Rd LBUZ LU7 .... 83 K3
NPAG MK16 .... 16 B5
RMKS/WB MK17 .... 52 D6 ⑥
RMKS/WB MK17 .... 63 J1
RMKS/WB MK17 .... 64 C1
RMKS/WB MK17 .... 70 C5
TOW NN12 .... 11 J1
Church Sq LBUZ LU7 .... 84 A3
Church St BDWL MK13 .... 24 C6
BUCK/WIN MK18 .... 43 J6
BUCK/WIN MK18 .... 55 F3
BUCK/WIN MK18 .... 74 A3 ⑥
LBUZ LU7 .... 84 B1
RMKS/WB MK17 .... 53 F4
RMKS/WB MK17 .... 66 E2
STSTR MK11 .... 34 E2
WEAT MK2 .... 62 D2
WOLV MK12 .... 23 K6
Church Vw NPAG MK16 .... 26 C1
TOW NN12 .... 4 A1
Church Wk BTCHLY MK3 .... 61 J4
BUCK/WIN MK18 .... 74 A3 ⑥
LBUZ LU7 .... 85 J2
RBEDW MK43 .... 29 H5
Church Wy TOW NN12 .... 8 E6
Cinnamon Gv WTR/OFPK MK7 .. 51 F4 ⑥
Clare Crs TOW NN12 .... 4 E4
Claremont Av STSTR MK11 .... 35 F3
Clarence Rd LBUZ LU7 .... 84 B1
STSTR MK11 .... 35 F2
Claredon Dr CNH/GTH/TM MK8 .. 36 C5
Claridge Dr MKV MK10 .... 39 F5
Clark Crs TOW NN12 .... 5 F1
Clarke Rd DBGH MK1 .... 50 B5
Claycutters BUCK/WIN MK18 .. 74 B3 ⑥
Clay HI CNH/GTH/TM MK8 .... 36 B5
Clayton Ga GTLIN MK14 .... 25 K5
Cleavers Av GTLIN MK14 .... 2 D2
Cleeve Crs BTCHLY MK3 .... 61 K1
Clegg Sq SHEN MK5 .... 48 E5
Clerkenwell PI
EAG/OLD/WT MK6 .... 38 A5 ⑥
Cleveland Cl BDWL MK13 .... 36 E1
Cleveland Dr LBUZ LU7 .... 83 H1
Clifford Av WEAT MK2 .... 62 B4
Cline Ct CNH/GTH/TM MK8 ... 48 B3
Clipstone Crs LBUZ LU7 ...... 84 D2
Cloebury Paddock
WLLN MK15 .... 38 B4 ⑥
The Close BDWL MK13 .... 36 D3
RMKS/WB MK17 .... 66 C2
Cloudberry WTR/OFPK MK7 .. 51 F3 ⑥
Cloutsham Cl EMV/FZ MK4.... 61 F1
Clover Cl SHEN MK5 .... 48 D5
Cluny Ct WTR/OFPK MK7 ...... 51 J3 ⑥
Clydesdale PI GTLIN MK14 .... 37 K1 ⑥
Coachmaker Ct GTLIN MK14 .. 37 K1 ⑥
Cobb Hall Rd RMKS/WB MK17 .... 69 F2
Coberley Cl WLLN MK15 .... 38 A1
Cobham Cl BUCK/WIN MK18 .. 55 F2
Cochran Cl CNH/GTH/TM MK8 .. 48 B2
Cockerell Gv SHEN MK5 .... 49 F4
Coddimoor La RMKS/WB MK17 .. 59 J4
Cogan Ct CNH/GTH/TM MK8 .. 48 B2 ②
Coggeshall Gv WTR/OFPK MK7 .. 51 H2
Coldeaton La EMV/FZ MK4..... 48 E6
Coleridge Ct BTCHLY MK3 .... 61 K4
NPAG MK16 .... 25 J1 ③
Colesbourne Dr WLLN MK15 .. 37 K1
Coleshill PI BDWL MK13 .... 2 B2
Colgrain St GTLIN MK14 .... 37 J3
College Rd RBEDW MK43 ...... 29 F3
Colley HI BDWL MK13 .... 36 D3

Colne EAG/OLD/WT MK6 ...... 50 C3
Colston Bassett EMV/FZ MK4 .... 61 F2
Coltsfoot PI GTLIN MK14 .... 2 D2
Colts Holm Rd WOLV MK12 .... 23 K5
Columba Dr LBUZ LU7 .... 84 D1
Columbia PI CMK MK9 .... 3 J3
Combe Martin EMV/FZ MK4 .... 49 C6
Comfrey Ct WTR/OFPK MK7 .... 51 F4
Common La BDWL MK13 .... 36 D5
Concord Wy LBUZ LU7 .... 85 F4
Concra Pk RMKS/WB MK17 ... 52 D5 ⑥
Condor Cl EAG/OLD/WT MK6 .. 49 K2
Congreve Rd EAG/OLD/WT MK6 .. 50 C4
Coniston Rd LBUZ LU7 .... 83 H2
Coniston Wy WEAT MK2 .... 62 C5 ⑥
Conniburrow Bvd GTLIN MK14 .... 2 E1
Constable Cl GTLIN MK14 ..... 25 J6 ⑧
Constantine Wy BDWL MK13 .. 36 C2 ②
Conway Crs BTCHLY MK3 ..... 61 H3
Cook Cl WTR/OFPK MK7 .... 51 F5
Cooks La RMKS/WB MK17 ..... 76 B1
Coopers Ms GTLIN MK14 ...... 37 J1
Coots Cl BUCK/WIN MK18 .... 55 H4
Copeland Cl WTR/OFPK MK7 .. 51 H4
Copes Hvn SHEN MK5 .... 48 E6
Copper Beech Wy LBUZ LU7 .. 80 B5
Coppin La BDWL MK13 .... 36 D4
Copse Ga BUCK/WIN MK18 ... 74 B3
Corbet Ride LBUZ LU7 .... 83 J1
Corbett Cl WLLN MK15 .... 26 C6 ⑥
Cordwainer Ct GTLIN MK14 ... 37 J1 ⑥
Corfe Crs BTCHLY MK3 .... 61 J3
Coriander Ct WTR/OFPK MK7 .. 51 G4 ⑥
Corin Wy WEAT MK2 .... 62 C6
Cornbury Crs GTLIN MK14 .... 37 K1
Cornelia Cl WEAT MK2 .... 62 B5
Corn HI CNH/GTH/TM MK8 .... 36 B6
Cornwall Gv BTCHLY MK3 ..... 61 J2
Cornwalls Meadow
BUCK/WIN MK18 .... 55 G2
Coronation Rd RBEDW MK43... 29 J4
Corrigan Cl BTCHLY MK3 ...... 61 K3 ⑥
Corsham Ct CNH/GTH/TM MK8 .. 36 C6 ②
Cosgrove Rd RMKN MK19 ..... 22 C6
Cotefield Dr LBUZ LU7 .... 80 B5
Cotes Wy LBUZ LU7 .... 82 E6
Cotman Cl WOLV MK12 .... 35 J2 ⑥
Cotswold Dr LBUZ LU7 .... 83 H1
Cottesloe Cl LBUZ LU7 .... 82 D6 ⑥
Cottesloe Ct STSTR MK11 .... 35 G2 ⑥
Cottingham Gv BTCHLY MK3 .. 61 K4
Cottisford Crs GTLIN MK14 ... 25 H4
Countisbury EMV/FZ MK4 ...... 61 G1
Courthouse Cl BUCK/WIN MK18 .. 74 A2
Court Rd RBEDW MK43 .... 29 J5
The Court RMKS/WB MK17 .... 40 E3 ⑥
Coverack PI EMV/FZ MK4 ...... 60 E3 ⑥
Coverdale BDWL MK13 .... 37 F2 ⑥
Cowdray Cl WLLN MK15 .... 38 B4
Cowper Cl NPAG MK16 .... 25 K1
Cox Gdns TOW NN12 .... 4 B1
Coxwell Cl BUCK/WIN MK18 .. 55 J2 ⑥
Craddocks Cl BDWL MK13 .... 36 E4
Craddocks Dr BDWL MK13 .... 80 B4
Craigmore Av BTCHLY MK3 ... 61 J3
Cranberry Cl WTR/OFPK MK7 .. 51 G3
Cranborne Av EMV/FZ MK4 ... 60 B1
Cranbrook RMKS/WB MK17 ... 52 C4
Crane Cl SHEN MK5 .... 36 E6
Crane Wy RBEDW MK43 .... 29 K3
Cranfield Rd NPAG MK16 ...... 27 K5
RMKS/WB MK17 .... 40 E1
Cranwell Cl SHEN MK5 .... 48 E6
The Craven BDWL MK13 .... 2 A1
Crawley Rd RBEDW MK43 ...... 27 H1
RMKS/WB MK17 .... 65 G3
Creed St WOLV MK12 .... 24 A6
The Crescent RMKN MK19 .... 24 B3
TOW NN12 .... 9 F6
WEAT MK2 .... 62 B2
Creslow Ct STSTR MK11 ...... 35 G2
Cressey Av SHEN MK5 .... 48 E5
Cricketers Rw BUCK/WIN MK18... 74 B3
Cricklebeck BDWL MK13 .... 36 E2
Crispin Rd BDWL MK13 .... 24 E6
Crofts End NPAG MK16 .... 16 E2
Crofts La RMKS/WB MK17 ..... 69 G2
Cromarty Ct BTCHLY MK3 ..... 49 H6
Cromwell Av NPAG MK16 ...... 25 K2
Cromwell Ct BUCK/WIN MK18 .. 55 H1 ⑥
Cropredy Ct BUCK/WIN MK18 .. 55 H1 ⑥
Cropwell Bishop EMV/FZ MK4.. 61 F2
Crosby Ct CNH/GTH/TM MK8 .. 48 B3
Cross Bucks Wy LBUZ LU7 .... 79 H4
Cross End RMKS/WB MK17 ... 52 A1
Crosshills STSTR MK11 .... 34 E3
Crosslands GTLIN MK14 .... 25 G5
Cross St NPAG MK16 .... 26 B1 ⑥

Cross Tree Rd RMKN MK19..... 33 F4
Crossway LBUZ LU7 .... 84 D2
Crowborough La WTR/OFPK MK7.. 51 F1
Crow La RBEDW MK43 .... 53 J5
RMKS/WB MK17 .... 52 C1
Crowther Ct SHEN MK5 .... 49 F4
Croxley Cl LBUZ LU7 .... 84 A1 ⑥
Croydon Cl EMV/FZ MK4........ 49 F6
Cruickshank Gv
CNH/GTH/TM MK8 .... 48 A1
Crummock PI WEAT MK2 .... 62 C5
Cuff La RMKS/WB MK17 .... 71 H4
Culbertson La BDWL MK13..... 36 B1
Cullen PI WEAT MK2 .... 62 C6
Culmstock Ct EMV/FZ MK4 ... 61 G1 ⑥
Culrain PI WOLV MK12 .... 36 A3
Culross Gv MKV MK10 .... 39 F5
Cumbria Cl BTCHLY MK3 .... 61 J2
Currier Dr GTLIN MK14 .... 37 H1
Curtis Cft SHEN MK5 .... 48 E6
Curzon PI WTR/OFPK MK7 ..... 51 K5
Cutlers Ms GTLIN MK14 .... 37 J1 ⑧
Cutlers Wy LBUZ LU7 .... 84 C3
Cygnus Dr LBUZ LU7 .... 84 E1 ⑥
Cypress NPAG MK16 .... 25 K2

D

Dalgin PI CMK MK9 .... 3 K3
Dalton Ga MKV MK10 .... 38 E4
Dalvina PI WOLV MK12 .... 36 A3
Dane Rd DBGH MK1 .... 62 C1
Danesbrook Cl EMV/FZ MK4 ... 49 G5
Danes Wy LBUZ LU7 .... 84 E2
Daniels Welch EAG/OLD/WT MK6 .. 49 K3
Dansteed Wy BDWL MK13 .... 2 B1
CNH/GTH/TM MK8 .... 36 B6
CNH/GTH/TM MK8 .... 48 A2
GTLIN MK14 .... 37 J2
Darin Ct CNH/GTH/TM MK8 .... 48 B1
Darley Ga GTLIN MK14 .... 37 J2
Darnel Cl EAG/OLD/WT MK6 .... 49 K4
Dart Cl NPAG MK16 .... 26 C1 ⑥
Daubeney Ga SHEN MK5 ...... 48 C3
Davenport Lea
WTR/OFPK MK7 .... 51 K4 ⑥
Davy Av SHEN MK5 .... 49 F2
Dawson Rd DBGH MK1 .... 50 B6
Daylesford Ct WLLN MK15 .... 38 A2 ⑥
Dean Farm La LBUZ LU7 .... 78 D2
Dean Rd LBUZ LU7 .... 76 C6
Deanshanger Dr TOW NN12 .. 20 D5
Deanshanger Rd RMKN MK19 .. 33 G4
Dean's Rd WOLV MK12 .... 23 K6
Debbs Cl STSTR MK11 .... 35 F2
Deben Cl NPAG MK16 .... 26 D2 ②
De Clare Ct BUCK/WIN MK18 .. 55 H2 ⑥
Deepdale BDWL MK13 .... 37 F2 ⑧
Deerfern Cl GTLIN MK14 .... 25 H4
Deerfield Cl BUCK/WIN MK18 .. 55 H4 ②
Deethe Cl RMKS/WB MK17 .... 52 B3
Delamere Gdns LBUZ LU7 ..... 83 H2
Delaware Dr WLLN MK15 .... 26 A5
Delius Ct WTR/OFPK MK7 ...... 51 H5
The Dell LBUZ LU7 .... 80 C2
Deltic Av BDWL MK13 .... 36 E5
Demoram Cl BUCK/WIN MK18 .. 74 A4
Denbigh Hall Dr BTCHLY MK3 .. 49 J6
Denbigh Rd DBGH MK1 .... 62 A1
Denbigh Wy WEAT MK2 .... 62 B2 ⑥
Denchworth Ct EMV/FZ MK4 .. 61 F1 ②
Dene Cl BUCK/WIN MK18 ...... 74 B4 ⑥
RMKS/WB MK17 .... 52 D6
Denham Cl BTCHLY MK3 .... 61 G3
Denison Ct RMKS/WB MK17 .. 51 J3
Denmark St WEAT MK2 .... 62 C3
Denmead CNH/GTH/TM MK8 .. 36 B5
Dere PI WEAT MK2 .... 70 D1
Derwent Cl NPAG MK16 .... 26 C1 ②
Derwent Dr BTCHLY MK3 ...... 61 H3
Derwent Rd LBUZ LU7 .... 83 G2
Develin Cl GTLIN MK14 .... 25 J6 ②
Dexter Av EAG/OLD/WT MK6 .. 49 J1
Dickens Dr RMKN MK19 .... 34 C1
Dickens Rd WOLV MK12 .... 23 K5
Diddington Cl WEAT MK2 ...... 70 B2 ⑥
Digby Rd LBUZ LU7 .... 84 B1
Dingle Dell LBUZ LU7 .... 80 A5
Dixie La WTR/OFPK MK7 .... 51 H3
Docklewell Cl TOW NN12 .... 4 D4
Dodkin EAG/OLD/WT MK6 ..... 50 A4
Dodman Gn EMV/FZ MK4 ...... 60 E3
Doggett St LBUZ LU7 .... 84 B2 ⑥
Dolben Ct WLLN MK15 .... 26 C5
Donlee Furlong LBUZ LU7 ..... 84 D2
Donnington BDWL MK13 .... 36 E1

The Don *BTCHLY* MK3 ..... 61 G2
Doon Wy *WEAT* MK2 ..... 62 B6
Dorchester Av *BTCHLY* MK3 ..... 61 J1
Doreen Cl *WEAT* MK2 ..... 62 B4
Dorking Pl *SHEN* MK5 ..... 48 E5
Dormer Av *LBUZ* LU7 ..... 82 D6
Dorney Pl *BDWL* MK13 ..... 2 A3
Dorset Cl *BTCHLY* MK3 ..... 61 H2
Dorton Cl *CNH/GTH/TM* MK8 ..... 36 C6
Douglas Pl *EAG/OLD/WT* MK6 ..... 49 H1
Dove Cl *BUCK/WIN* MK18 ..... 55 H4
  NPAG MK16 ..... 26 C1
  TOW NN12 ..... 5 F6
Dovecote *NPAG* MK16 ..... 26 B1
Dove House Cl *BUCK/WIN* MK18 ..... 74 B3
Dover Ga *BTCHLY* MK3 ..... 61 J4
Dove Tree Rd *LBUZ* LU7 ..... 84 D1
Downdean *EAG/OLD/WT* MK6 ..... 49 K1
Downer Cl *BUCK/WIN* MK18 ..... 55 J3
Downham Rd *RMKS/WB* MK17 ..... 52 D5
Downland *CNH/GTH/TM* MK8 ..... 36 B5
Downley Av *BDWL* MK13 ..... 2 B2
Downs Barn Bvd *GTLIN* MK14 ..... 37 J3
Downs Vw *RMKS/WB* MK17 ..... 63 H1
Drakeloe Cl *RMKS/WB* MK17 ..... 65 G3
Drakes Ms *CNH/GTH/TM* MK8 ..... 48 B2
Drakewell Rd *RMKS/WB* MK17 ..... 63 J2
Drayton Rd *WTR/OFPK* MK7 ..... 69 F3
  WEAT MK2 ..... 62 B6
The Drive *RBEDW* MK43 ..... 28 E3
Drovers Wy *RMKS/WB* MK17 ..... 69 G3
Drummond Hay *WLLN* MK15 ..... 26 B6
Dryden Cl *NPAG* MK16 ..... 25 K1
Dryden Rd *TOW* NN12 ..... 5 F4
Duchess Gv *WTR/OFPK* MK7 ..... 51 H2
Duck End *RMKS/WB* MK17 ..... 71 J4
Duck Lake *BUCK/WIN* MK18 ..... 43 H5
Duck Lake Cl *BUCK/WIN* MK18 ..... 43 H5
Duck La *RMKS/WB* MK17 ..... 65 G4
Dudley Hl *SHEN* MK5 ..... 48 D3
Dudley St *LBUZ* LU7 ..... 84 B3
Dukes Dr *WEAT* MK2 ..... 62 B2
Dukes Piece *BUCK/WIN* MK18 ..... 55 J3
Dukes Ride *LBUZ* LU7 ..... 79 K4
Duke St *RMKS/WB* MK17 ..... 52 E5
Dulverton Dr *EMV/FZ* MK4 ..... 49 G6
Dulwich Cl *NPAG* MK16 ..... 26 B3
Dumfries Cl *BTCHLY* MK3 ..... 49 J6
Dunbar Cl *BTCHLY* MK3 ..... 61 G2
Duncan Gv *SHEN* MK5 ..... 48 C3
Duncan Rd *RBEDW* MK43 ..... 29 F3
Dunchurch Dl *WTR/OFPK* MK7 ..... 51 G4
Duncombe Dr *LBUZ* LU7 ..... 84 B3
Duncombe St *WEAT* MK2 ..... 62 A4
Dunkery Beacon *EMV/FZ* MK4 ..... 49 G6
Dunsby Rd *EAG/OLD/WT* MK6 ..... 49 K5
Dunster Ct *EMV/FZ* MK4 ..... 49 H6
Dunvedin Pl *WOLV* MK12 ..... 36 A3
Dunvegan Cl *WEAT* MK2 ..... 70 C1
Duparc Cl *WTR/OFPK* MK7 ..... 51 G4
Durrans Ct *WEAT* MK2 ..... 62 D2
Durrell Cl *LBUZ* LU7 ..... 83 K2
Dyersdale *BDWL* MK13 ..... 37 F2
Dyers Ms *GTLIN* MK14 ..... 37 J1

E

Eaglestone *EAG/OLD/WT* MK6 ..... 49 K1
Earls Cl *WEAT* MK2 ..... 62 A3
Earls Willow *BDWL* MK13 ..... 24 D5
Easby Gv *WTR/OFPK* MK7 ..... 39 F6
Eastbury Ct *EMV/FZ* MK4 ..... 61 G2
East Chapel *EMV/FZ* MK4 ..... 60 E3
East Dales *BDWL* MK13 ..... 37 F2
Eastern Wy *LBUZ* LU7 ..... 80 C3
Eastfield Crs *TOW* NN12 ..... 12 A6
East Hills *RBEDW* MK43 ..... 29 J5
East Rd *RBEDW* MK43 ..... 28 E3
East St *LBUZ* LU7 ..... 84 C1
Ebbsgrove *SHEN* MK5 ..... 36 E6
Eddington St *EMV/FZ* MK4 ..... 61 G2
Edgecote *CNH/GTH/TM* MK8 ..... 48 D1
Edge Hill Ct *BUCK/WIN* MK18 ..... 55 H1
Edison Sq *SHEN* MK5 ..... 49 F4
Edmonds Cl *BUCK/WIN* MK18 ..... 55 J2
Edmund Cl *SHEN* MK5 ..... 48 C2
Edrich Av *EAG/OLD/WT* MK6 ..... 49 J1
Edward St *LBUZ* LU7 ..... 84 B1
Edwin Cl *RMKS/WB* MK17 ..... 63 J1
Edy Ct *SHEN* MK5 ..... 36 D6
Eelbrook Av *BDWL* MK13 ..... 2 A4
Egerton Ga *SHEN* MK5 ..... 48 D5
Egmont Av *STSTR* MK11 ..... 35 F3
Eider Cl *BUCK/WIN* MK18 ..... 55 H3
Elder Ga *CMK* MK9 ..... 2 B7
Eleanor Cl *RMKS/WB* MK17 ..... 65 G4

Elfords *EAG/OLD/WT* MK6 ..... 49 K3
Elgar Gv *WTR/OFPK* MK7 ..... 51 H4
Eliot Cl *NPAG* MK16 ..... 15 J6
Ellenstow *BDWL* MK13 ..... 36 D3
Ellerburn Pl *EMV/FZ* MK4 ..... 48 E6
Ellesborough Gv
  CNH/GTH/TM MK8 ..... 36 A4
Ellisgill Ct *BDWL* MK13 ..... 36 E3
Elm Cl *RMKS/WB* MK17 ..... 69 F3
Elm Dr *RMKN* MK19 ..... 33 J3
Elmers Cl *RMKN* MK19 ..... 46 B3
Elmers Pk *BTCHLY* MK3 ..... 61 K3
Elmfield Cl *TOW* NN12 ..... 21 J2
Elmfields Ga *BUCK/WIN* MK18 ..... 74 B3
Elm Gv *RMKS/WB* MK17 ..... 52 C5
Elmhurst Cl *EMV/FZ* MK4 ..... 49 J5
Elmridge Ct *EMV/FZ* MK4 ..... 61 F1
Elmside *BUCK/WIN* MK18 ..... 74 B3
The Elms *BTCHLY* MK3 ..... 61 H1
Elm St *BUCK/WIN* MK18 ..... 55 G3
Elthorne Wy *NPAG* MK16 ..... 26 B3
Elton *EAG/OLD/WT* MK6 ..... 50 C2
Emerton Gdns *STSTR* MK11 ..... 34 E2
Emmett Cl *EMV/FZ* MK4 ..... 61 F2
Empingham Cl *WEAT* MK2 ..... 70 C1
Emu Cl *LBUZ* LU7 ..... 80 B2
Enfield Cha *GTLIN* MK14 ..... 37 G2
Engaine Dr *SHEN* MK5 ..... 48 C3
Enmore Ga *CMK* MK9 ..... 3 K2
Ennell Gv *WEAT* MK2 ..... 62 B6
Ennerdale Cl *WEAT* MK2 ..... 62 C5
Enterprise La *CMK* MK9 ..... 3 K3
Enterprise Wy *LBUZ* LU7 ..... 84 B4
Epsom Cl *LBUZ* LU7 ..... 83 J3
Epsom Gv *BTCHLY* MK3 ..... 61 C5
Eriboll Cl *LBUZ* LU7 ..... 83 G3
Erica Rd *WOLV* MK12 ..... 36 B3
Eridge Gn *WTR/OFPK* MK7 ..... 51 F1
Esk Wy *BTCHLY* MK3 ..... 61 G2
Essendon Ct *STSTR* MK11 ..... 35 G2
Essex Cl *BTCHLY* MK3 ..... 61 J2
Eston Ct *BDWL* MK13 ..... 36 D2
Etheridge Av *MKV* MK10 ..... 51 H1
Ethorpe *CNH/GTH/TM* MK8 ..... 36 B6
Eton Crs *WOLV* MK12 ..... 35 K1
Evans Ga *EAG/OLD/WT* MK6 ..... 49 H1
Evelyn Pl *BDWL* MK13 ..... 24 D6
Everley Cl *EMV/FZ* MK4 ..... 48 E6
Exebridge *EMV/FZ* MK4 ..... 49 F6
Exmoor Ga *EMV/FZ* MK4 ..... 61 H1
Eynsham Ct *WLLN* MK15 ..... 38 B5

F

Fadmoor Pl *EMV/FZ* MK4 ..... 49 F6
Fairfax *BDWL* MK13 ..... 36 E1
Fairfield Rd *TOW* NN12 ..... 10 A3
Fairford Crs *GTLIN* MK14 ..... 37 K1
Fair Meadow *BUCK/WIN* MK18 ..... 74 B3
Fairways *BDWL* MK13 ..... 35 K5
Falcon Av *EAG/OLD/WT* MK6 ..... 3 K4
Falcon Vw *TOW* NN12 ..... 4 A1
Fallowfield *LBUZ* LU7 ..... 84 D2
Falmouth Pl *EAG/OLD/WT* MK6 ..... 3 H7
Faraday Dr *SHEN* MK5 ..... 49 F5
Farinton *CNH/GTH/TM* MK8 ..... 36 C5
Farjeon Ct *WTR/OFPK* MK7 ..... 51 J5
Farmborough *EAG/OLD/WT* MK6 ..... 50 B3
Farnham Ct *CNH/GTH/TM* MK8 ..... 36 B6
Farrier Pl *GTLIN* MK14 ..... 37 J1
Farthing Gv *EAG/OLD/WT* MK6 ..... 50 B3
Faulkner's Wy *LBUZ* LU7 ..... 84 A2
Favell Dr *EMV/FZ* MK4 ..... 49 H5
Featherstone Rd *WOLV* MK12 ..... 35 H2
Fegans Ct *STSTR* MK11 ..... 34 E1
Felbridge *WTR/OFPK* MK7 ..... 51 F2
Fences La *NPAG* MK16 ..... 15 K1
Fennel Dr *GTLIN* MK14 ..... 37 H3
Fennymere *CNH/GTH/TM* MK8 ..... 36 A6
Fenny Rd *RMKS/WB* MK17 ..... 70 D5
Fenton Ct *CNH/GTH/TM* MK8 ..... 48 C1
Fernan Dell *CNH/GTH/TM* MK8 ..... 48 A2
Fernborough Hvn
  EMV/FZ MK4 ..... 61 F1
Ferndale *EAG/OLD/WT* MK6 ..... 38 A6
Fern Gv *WEAT* MK2 ..... 62 B6
Field Cl *MKV* MK10 ..... 17 F1
Field La *WOLV* MK12 ..... 35 J2
Finch Cl *MKV* MK10 ..... 38 E4
Finch Crs *LBUZ* LU7 ..... 83 K4
Findlay Wy *WEAT* MK2 ..... 62 B3
Fingle Dr *BDWL* MK13 ..... 24 B6
Finmere Wy *LBUZ* LU7 ..... 84 B4
Fire La *RMKS/WB* MK17 ..... 69 G2
Firs Pth *LBUZ* LU7 ..... 80 B6
First Av *DBGH* MK1 ..... 62 B2

Fishermead Bvd
  EAG/OLD/WT MK6 ..... 3 J7
Fishers Fld *BUCK/WIN* MK18 ..... 55 F3
Fishweir *LBUZ* LU7 ..... 77 G6
Flambard Cl *WLLN* MK15 ..... 25 K6
Flaxley Ga *MKV* MK10 ..... 39 F5
Fleet Cl *BUCK/WIN* MK18 ..... 55 J1
The Fleet *EAG/OLD/WT* MK6 ..... 38 A5
Fleming Dr *EAG/OLD/WT* MK6 ..... 50 A3
Fletchers Ms *GTLIN* MK14 ..... 37 J1
Flitton Ct *STSTR* MK11 ..... 35 G2
Flora Thompson Dr *NPAG* MK16 ..... 15 J5
Florin Cl *WLLN* MK15 ..... 25 K6
Folly Farm *RBEDW* MK43 ..... 29 H5
Folly Rd *RMKN* MK19 ..... 33 J3
Fontwell Dr *RMKS/WB* MK17 ..... 61 F6
Forches Cl *EMV/FZ* MK4 ..... 61 G1
Fordcombe Lea
  WTR/OFPK MK7 ..... 51 G1
Ford St *BUCK/WIN* MK18 ..... 55 G3
Forest Ri *EAG/OLD/WT* MK6 ..... 50 A1
Forfar Dr *BTCHLY* MK3 ..... 61 J1
Formby Cl *BTCHLY* MK3 ..... 61 F4
Fortescue Dr *SHEN* MK5 ..... 48 D3
Fortuna Ct *WTR/OFPK* MK7 ..... 51 H3
Foscote Rd *EAG/OLD/WT* MK6 ..... 43 J6
Foscott Wy *BUCK/WIN* MK18 ..... 55 H1
Fosters La *BDWL* MK13 ..... 2 A3
Founders Ms *GTLIN* MK14 ..... 37 J1
Fountaine Cl *GTLIN* MK14 ..... 25 H6
Fowler *GTLIN* MK14 ..... 25 F6
Foxcovert Rd *SHEN* MK5 ..... 48 C5
Foxgate *NPAG* MK16 ..... 26 A1
Foxglove Ct *NPAG* MK16 ..... 25 J1
Foxhunter Dr *GTLIN* MK14 ..... 37 G1
Foxton *EAG/OLD/WT* MK6 ..... 50 C3
Fox Wy *BUCK/WIN* MK18 ..... 55 H4
Framlingham Ct *SHEN* MK5 ..... 48 D4
France Furlong *GTLIN* MK14 ..... 25 J5
Francis Ct *SHEN* MK5 ..... 48 D3
Frank Atter Cft *WOLV* MK12 ..... 35 K2
Franklins Cft *WOLV* MK12 ..... 35 K2
Frankston Av *STSTR* MK11 ..... 35 F2
Freeman Cl *WOLV* MK12 ..... 35 J2
Frensham Dr *WEAT* MK2 ..... 62 B4
Friary Gdns *NPAG* MK16 ..... 26 B3
Friday St *LBUZ* LU7 ..... 84 B2
Frithwood Crs *WTR/OFPK* MK7 ..... 51 G1
Frog Hall *TOW* NN12 ..... 8 A6
Froxfield Ct *EMV/FZ* MK4 ..... 61 F2
Fryday St *EAG/OLD/WT* MK6 ..... 49 H2
Fulmer St *CNH/GTH/TM* MK8 ..... 48 A2
  EMV/FZ MK4 ..... 49 F6
  SHEN MK5 ..... 48 E5
Fulwoods Dr *EAG/OLD/WT* MK6 ..... 49 K1
Furness Crs *BTCHLY* MK3 ..... 61 J2
Furtho La *TOW* NN12 ..... 21 K2
Fury Ct *CNH/GTH/TM* MK8 ..... 48 B2
Fyfield Barrow *WTR/OFPK* MK7 ..... 51 H3
Fyne Dr *LBUZ* LU7 ..... 83 H1

G

The Gables *LBUZ* LU7 ..... 83 K3
Gable Thorne *WTR/OFPK* MK7 ..... 51 J3
Gabriel Cl *WTR/OFPK* MK7 ..... 51 H4
Gaddesden Crs
  WTR/OFPK MK7 ..... 51 H2
Gadsden Cl *RBEDW* MK43 ..... 29 K3
Gadsden Ct *RMKS/WB* MK17 ..... 70 D5
Gairloch Av *WEAT* MK2 ..... 62 C6
Gallagher Cl
  CNH/GTH/TM MK8 ..... 48 B1
Galley Hl *STSTR* MK11 ..... 35 G3
Galley La *RMKS/WB* MK17 ..... 63 F6
Galloway Cl *BTCHLY* MK3 ..... 61 H1
Ganton Cl *BTCHLY* MK3 ..... 61 G2
Garamonde Dr
  CNH/GTH/TM MK8 ..... 36 B4
Garbo Cl *CNH/GTH/TM* MK8 ..... 48 A2
Garden Hedge *LBUZ* LU7 ..... 84 B1
Garden Leys *LBUZ* LU7 ..... 84 D3
Gardner Ct *BDWL* MK13 ..... 36 B2
Garland Ct *CNH/GTH/TM* MK8 ..... 48 B1
Garraways *EAG/OLD/WT* MK6 ..... 49 K3
Garston *CNH/GTH/TM* MK8 ..... 36 C5
Garthwaite Crs *SHEN* MK5 ..... 48 C6
Gatcombe *CNH/GTH/TM* MK8 ..... 48 A2
Gatewick La *WTR/OFPK* MK7 ..... 51 F6
Gawcott Rd *BUCK/WIN* MK18 ..... 54 E6
Gayal Cft *SHEN* MK5 ..... 48 E5
Gemini Cl *LBUZ* LU7 ..... 84 E1
George St *LBUZ* LU7 ..... 84 C2

  RMKS/WB MK17
  WEAT MK2
Gerard Cl *BDWL* MK13
Germander Pl *GTLIN* MK14
Gershwin Ct *WTR/OFPK* MK7
Gibbwin *GTLIN* MK14
Gibsons Gn *BDWL* MK13
Giffard Rd *WEAT* MK2
Gifford Ga *GTLIN* MK14
Gifford Pl *BUCK/WIN* MK18
Gig La *LBUZ* LU7
Gilbert Cl *BTCHLY* MK3
Gilbert Scott Ct *TOW* NN12
Gilbert Scott Rd *BUCK/WIN* MK18
Gilders Ms *GTLIN* MK14
Gillamoor Cl *EMV/FZ* MK4
Gisburn Cl *BDWL* MK13
Gladstone Cl *NPAG* MK16
Glamorgan Cl *BTCHLY* MK3
Glazier Dr *GTLIN* MK14
Glebe Cl *BUCK/WIN* MK18
  SHEN MK5
Glebe Rd *RMKN* MK19
Glebe Ter *BUCK/WIN* MK18
Gledfield Pl *WOLV* MK12
Gleeman Cl *WOLV* MK12
Gleneagles Cl *BTCHLY* MK3
Globe La *LBUZ* LU7
Gloucester Rd *WOLV* MK12
Glovers La *BDWL* MK13
Glyn St *BDWL* MK13
Glynswood Rd *BUCK/WIN* MK18
Goathland Cft *EMV/FZ* MK4
Godwin Cl *WTR/OFPK* MK7
Golden Dr *EAG/OLD/WT* MK6
Golden Riddy *LBUZ* LU7
Goldilocks *WTR/OFPK* MK7
Goldmark Cl *WTR/OFPK* MK7
Golspie Cft *WOLV* MK12
Goodman Gdns
  EAG/OLD/WT MK6
Goodwick Gv *EMV/FZ* MK4
Goodwood *CNH/GTH/TM* MK8
Goran Av *STSTR* MK11
Gordale *BDWL* MK13
Goring *GTLIN* MK14
Gorman Pl *WEAT* MK2
Gorricks *STSTR* MK11
Goslington *DBGH* MK1
Goudhurst Ct *WTR/OFPK* MK7
Grace Av *EAG/OLD/WT* MK6
Graces Cl *RBEDW* MK43
Grafham Cl *GTLIN* MK14
Grafton Cl *TOW* NN12
Grafton Ga *CMK* MK9
Grafton Rd *TOW* NN12
Grafton St *BDWL* MK13
  DBGH MK1
  EAG/OLD/WT MK6
  RMKN MK19
Grafton Wy *TOW* NN12
Graham Hl *TOW* NN12
Graham Hill Rd *TOW* NN12
Grampian Ga *EAG/OLD/WT* MK6
Gramwell *SHEN* MK5
Grand Union Canal Wk
  BDWL MK13
  GTLIN MK14
  LBUZ LU7
  RMKS/WB MK17
  TOW NN12
  WLLN MK15
  WOLV MK12
Granes End *LBUZ* LU7
Grange Cl *BUCK/WIN* MK18
  LBUZ LU7
Grange Gdns *LBUZ* LU7
Grange Rd *BTCHLY* MK3
Grantham Ct *SHEN* MK5
Granville Sq *WLLN* MK15
Grasmere Wy *LBUZ* LU7
  WEAT MK2
Grasscroft *EMV/FZ* MK4
Grassington *BDWL* MK13
Graveney Pl *EAG/OLD/WT* MK6
Grays Cl *TOW* NN12
Grays La *TOW* NN12
  TOW NN12
Great Brickhill La
  RMKS/WB MK17
Greatchesters *BDWL* MK13
Great Denson *EAG/OLD/WT* MK6
Great Gnd *GTLIN* MK14
Greatheed Dell *WTR/OFPK* MK7
Great Horwood Rd
  RMKS/WB MK17
Great Linch *MKV* MK10

...onks St
...GTH/TM MK8 .... 36 B4
...MK12 .... 35 J2
...ade *BUCK/WIN* MK18 .... 55 G5
.. Wy *LBUZ* LU7 .... 84 E3 🔲
...arm Rd *NPAG* MK16 ...... 26 B1
...eld Rd *NPAG* MK16 ...... 25 K1
.. *LBUZ* LU7 .... 80 B6
.. Cl *SHEN* MK5 .... 48 D1 🔲
...nds *LBUZ* LU7 .... 84 D1
...nds Rd *NPAG* MK16 ...... 25 K2 🔲
...a *RMKS/WB* MK17........ 53 F6
...N12 .... 4 D4
...N12 .... 18 A1
...w Pl *BTCHLY* MK3 .... 49 K6 🔲
...ys La *WOLV* MK12 .... 35 K2
...ark Dr *NPAG* MK16 ...... 26 A2
...and Ridge Wk *LBUZ* LU7 ... 79 K6
.../WB MK17 .... 64 C6
...de Hl *EMV/FZ* MK4 ...... 60 E2
...en *BUCK/WIN* MK18 ...... 57 F3
.../LD/WT MK6................ 50 B1
.. ...MK13 .... 78 D4
.. *LBUZ* LU7 .... 26 B1
...V MK43...................... 29 F3
...MK19 .... 13 H1
...MK19 .... 23 G3
...MK19 .... 33 K3
.../WB MK17 .... 66 B2
...MK5 .... 48 D1
...N12 .... 10 A4
...ew Dr *TOW* NN12 .... 4 E3
...y *RMKS/WB* MK17.......... 69 C1
...ay *RMKS/WB* MK17 .... 66 B3
...ays *RMKS/WB* MK17 ...... 63 H1
...ch Gdns *NPAG* MK16 .... 26 A3 🔲
...s Dr *WTR/OFPK* MK7 ...... 51 H3
...e Rd *BUCK/WIN* MK18 ...... 55 F2
...nd La *BUCK/WIN* MK18 ... 74 B3
...s *EAG/OLD/WT* MK6 ...... 50 B1
...nley *EMV/FZ* MK4 .... 61 F1 🔲
...Ga *MKV* MK10 .... 39 F4
...*EAG/OLD/WT* MK6 ...... 49 K2 🔲
...rch *NPAG* MK16 .... 17 F1
...e Ct *WLLN* MK15 .... 26 B6 🔲
...e *BDWL* MK13 .... 36 E2
...ridge *WTR/OFPK* MK7 .... 51 F2
...nt Cl *EMV/FZ* MK4 ...... 60 E1
...el Cl *WTR/OFPK* MK7 .... 51 G3 🔲
...ry Place Est *LBUZ* LU7 .. 84 B3 🔲
...ry Rd *LBUZ* LU7 .... 84 B5
...*LBUZ* LU7 .... 84 B3
...l *LBUZ* LU7 .... 84 B3
...rook *RMKS/WB* MK17 .... 63 J1 🔲
...ve *BDWL* MK13 .... 36 D3
...y MK3 .... 61 K3
...e 26 A2
.../WB MK17 .... 52 C4
...ay *BTCHLY* MK3........... 49 K6
...LD/WT MK6.................. 50 E3
...OFPK MK7.................... 51 G3 🔲
...ins *BDWL* MK13 .... 24 E5 🔲
...*RMKS/WB* MK17 .... 53 C5 🔲
...Ct *EMV/FZ* MK4 .... 60 E1 🔲
...er Ct *GTLIN* MK14 ...... 37 J1
...*EMV/FZ* MK4 .... 60 E2
...s Av *EAG/OLD/WT* MK6 .... 3 J5
...Cl *SHEN* MK5.............. 48 D2
...Ct *WEAT* MK2.............. 70 B2

H

...y Md *BDWL* MK13 .... 36 E4 🔲
...ton Cl *BTCHLY* MK3 ...... 61 H1 🔲
...*CNH/GTH/TM* MK8 ...... 48 C1
...Pl *BDWL* MK13 .... 2 B3
...s Dr *BDWL* MK13 .... 36 C2
..: Av *GTLIN* MK14 .... 25 K4
...aite *CNH/GTH/TM* MK8 .. 36 A6
...*CNH/GTH/TM* MK8 ...... 36 B5
...*STSTR* MK11 .... 35 F2
...*UCK/WIN* MK18.......... 43 J6
...MK19 .... 34 C1
...*NPAG* MK16............... 17 H3
...Pl *MKV* MK10............. 39 F5
...hesters *BDWL* MK13 .... 36 C1
...*BDWL* MK13 .... 36 D3
...con Gv *EMV/FZ* MK4 ...... 60 E1
...La *RMKS/WB* MK17 ...... 61 F5
...*EAG/OLD/WT* MK6........ 49 J3
...wood Ga
...OFPK MK7.................... 51 F2
...nd Crs *WLLN* MK15 ...... 38 A1 🔲
...ire Cl *BTCHLY* MK3 ...... 61 J1 🔲
...Cl *BDWL* MK13 .... 36 D2

Hampton *CNH/GTH/TM* MK8 .... 48 C1
Hampton Court Cl *TOW* NN12 ...... 5 F4 🔲
Handel Md *WTR/OFPK* MK7 .... 51 K4
Handley Page Cl *RBEDW* MK43 .... 29 F3 🔲
Hanmer Rd *EAG/OLD/WT* MK6...... 50 D4
Hanover Ct *LBUZ* LU7 .... 83 J2
Hanscomb Cl *WLLN* MK15 .... 38 B5 🔲
Hanslope Circular Ride
    RMKN MK19 .... 12 C1
Hanslope Rd *RMKN* MK19.......... 13 G4
Harborne Ct
    CNH/GTH/TM MK8 .... 35 K5 🔲
Harby Cl *EMV/FZ* MK4 .... 61 F2
Harcourt *BDWL* MK13 .... 36 D4 🔲
Harcourt Cl *LBUZ* LU7 .... 83 K2
Harding Rd *MKV* MK10 .... 51 H1
Hardwick Ms *RMKS/WB* MK17 .... 52 C6
Hardwick Pl *RMKS/WB* MK17 .... 52 C5
Hardwick Rd *RMKS/WB* MK17 .... 52 C5
Harebell Cl *WTR/OFPK* MK7 ...... 51 G4
Hare Cl *BDWL* MK13 .... 55 H4
Hareden Cft *EMV/FZ* MK4 .... 60 E2
Haresmoor Dr *TOW* NN12 .... 5 F5
Hargreaves Nook *GTLIN* MK14.... 26 A3
Harkness Cl *WEAT* MK2 .... 62 C5 🔲
Harlans Cl *EAG/OLD/WT* MK6 .... 50 A1
Harlech Pl *BTCHLY* MK3.............. 61 K4
Harlequin Pl *SHEN* MK5 .... 48 C6 🔲
Harle Stone Ct *GTLIN* MK14 ...... 25 K4 🔲
Harmony Rw *LBUZ* LU7.............. 84 E4
Harnett Dr *WOLV* MK12 .... 35 G1
Harpers La *GTLIN* MK14............ 25 J5
Harrier Cl *EAG/OLD/WT* MK6 ...... 49 K1
Harrier Dr *EAG/OLD/WT* MK6 ...... 38 A6
Harrison Cl *SHEN* MK5 .... 49 G3
Harrowden *BDWL* MK13 .... 24 E6
Harrow Rd *LBUZ* LU7................ 84 C4
Hartdames *SHEN* MK5 .... 48 D6
Harter Av *RBEDW* MK43 .... 29 H6
Hartfield Cl *WTR/OFPK* MK7 ...... 51 F2
Hartland Av *EMV/FZ* MK4 .... 60 E3
Hartley *GTLIN* MK14................ 25 H5
Hartwell Crs *LBUZ* LU7 .... 84 C2
Hartwort Cl *WTR/OFPK* MK7 ...... 51 G3
Harvard Cl *GTLIN* MK14 .... 25 J3
Harvester Cl *WOLV* MK12 .... 35 J2
Harwood St *BDWL* MK13 .... 24 D6
Hasgill Ct *BDWL* MK13 .... 36 E2
Haslow Cl *CNH/GTH/TM* MK8 .... 36 B4 🔲
Hastings *STSTR* MK11 .... 35 F2
Hatchet Leys La *BUCK/WIN* MK18 .. 56 E3
Hatchlands *CNH/GTH/TM* MK8 .... 36 C6
Hatfield Av *RBEDW* MK43 .... 29 J6 🔲
Hathaway Ct
    CNH/GTH/TM MK8 .... 48 B1 🔲
Hatton *EAG/OLD/WT* MK6.......... 50 C3
Hauksbee Gdns *SHEN* MK5 .... 49 F4
Haversham Rd *RMKN* MK19 .... 24 A4
Hawkhurst Ga *WTR/OFPK* MK7 .. 50 E2 🔲
Hawkins Cl *STSTR* MK11 .... 34 E2 🔲
Hawkmoor Cl
    EAG/OLD/WT MK6................ 50 A1 🔲
Hawkridge *EMV/FZ* MK4............ 49 H6
Hawkwell Est *RMKN* MK19 .... 22 C6 🔲
Hawthorn Av *WEAT* MK2 .... 62 D3
Hawthorn Dr *TOW* NN12 .... 5 F1
Hawthorne Cl *LBUZ* LU7 .... 83 K1
The Hawthorns *RBEDW* MK43 .... 29 J4 🔲
    TOW NN12 .... 18 A2
Hawthorn Wy *LBUZ* LU7............ 82 D6 🔲
Haydock Cl *RMKS/WB* MK17 ...... 61 F5
Hayes Rd *RMKN* MK19................ 34 A2
Haynes Cl *RMKS/WB* MK17 .... 63 J1 🔲
Haythorp Cl *WLLN* MK15............ 38 A1
Haywood Pk *LBUZ* LU7 .... 77 F4 🔲
Hazel Crs *TOW* NN12 .... 4 E5
Hazel Gv *WEAT* MK2.................. 62 C4
Hazelhurst *EMV/FZ* MK4............ 60 E1
Hazelwood *GTLIN* MK14 .... 25 J5 🔲
Headingham Ct *SHEN* MK5 .... 48 D4 🔲
Heaney Cl *NPAG* MK16.............. 15 K6
Hearne Pl *EAG/OLD/WT* MK6 ...... 49 J1
Heath Cl *LBUZ* LU7 .... 79 K4
Heathcroft *GTLIN* MK14 .... 25 H6
Heathfield *WOLV* MK12 .... 36 B3
Heath Gn *LBUZ* LU7 .... 80 B3
Heath La *RMKS/WB* MK17.......... 64 B1
Heath Park Dr *LBUZ* LU7............ 80 B5
Heath Park Rd *LBUZ* LU7 .... 80 B4
Heath Rd *LBUZ* LU7 .... 80 B4
    RMKS/WB MK17 .... 71 J4
The Heath *LBUZ* LU7 .... 79 K4
Heathwood Cl *LBUZ* LU7............ 80 B4 🔲
The Hedgerows *EMV/FZ* MK4 ...... 49 H5
Hedges Ct *SHEN* MK5 .... 48 E3 🔲
Hele St *WTR/OFPK* MK7 .... 51 G6 🔲
Helford Pl *EAG/OLD/WT* MK6 ...... 3 K6
Helston Pl *EAG/OLD/WT* MK6...... 3 H7

Hemingway Cl *NPAG* MK16 .... 15 J6 🔲
Henders *STSTR* MK11 .... 35 F2
Hendrix Dr *CNH/GTH/TM* MK8.... 48 A2
Hengistbury La *EMV/FZ* MK4...... 60 C2
Henson Cl *RBEDW* MK43 .... 29 F3 🔲
Hepleswell *BDWL* MK13 .... 36 B6
Hercules Cl *LBUZ* LU7 .... 84 D1 🔲
Herdman Cl *WOLV* MK12 .... 35 J2 🔲
Heron Cl *TOW* NN12.................. 5 F6
Herriot Cl *NPAG* MK16 .... 15 K6
Hertford Pl *BTCHLY* MK3 .... 61 J1
Hesketh Crs *TOW* NN12.............. 5 F5
Hesketh Rd *TOW* NN12.............. 11 K5
Hetton Cl *BDWL* MK13................ 2 A1
Hexham Gdns *BTCHLY* MK3 .... 61 G5
Heybridge Crs *WTR/OFPK* MK7 .. 51 F6
Heydon Ct *BDWL* MK13 .... 24 D6 🔲
Hicks Ct *TOW* NN12.................. 5 G5
Hicks Rd *TOW* NN12.................. 5 F5
The Hide *EAG/OLD/WT* MK6 .... 50 B3
Higgs Ct *SHEN* MK5 .... 48 D1
High Banks *LBUZ* LU7 .... 85 K4
Highbury La *CMK* MK9 .... 3 J3
Highcroft *LBUZ* LU7 .... 84 D3 🔲
Highcroft Cl *TOW* NN12 .... 11 J5
Highfield Cl *BTCHLY* MK3 .... 61 K1
    NPAG MK16 .... 26 D1
Highfield Crs *RBEDW* MK43 .... 41 K6
Highfield Rd *BUCK/WIN* MK18 .... 74 A2
    LBUZ LU7 .... 84 D3
Highfields *TOW* NN12 .... 4 E5
Highgate Over *WTR/OFPK* MK7.... 51 G2
Highgrove Hl *CNH/GTH/TM* MK8.. 48 C1
High Halden *WTR/OFPK* MK7 ...... 51 G1 🔲
Highland Cl *BTCHLY* MK3 .... 49 J6
Highlands Rd *BUCK/WIN* MK18 .... 55 C1
High Rd *LBUZ* LU7.................... 78 D5
High St *BDWL* MK13 .... 24 C6
    BUCK/WIN MK18 .... 55 G3
    BUCK/WIN MK18 .... 57 F3
    BUCK/WIN MK18 .... 74 A3
    GTLIN MK14 .... 25 H4
    LBUZ LU7 .... 82 C5
    LBUZ LU7 .... 84 A3
    LBUZ LU7 .... 85 J2
    NPAG MK16 .... 16 E1
    NPAG MK16 .... 26 B1
    RBEDW MK43.................. 29 H5
    RMKN MK19 .... 13 H1
    RMKN MK19 .... 24 D2
    RMKN MK19 .... 33 K3
    RMKS/WB MK17 .... 52 C5
    RMKS/WB MK17 .... 58 D2
    RMKS/WB MK17 .... 59 J2
    RMKS/WB MK17 .... 65 G4
    RMKS/WB MK17 .... 66 A2
    STSTR MK11 .... 34 D1
    TOW NN12...................... 4 A1
    TOW NN12 .... 10 A3
    TOW NN12 .... 12 A5
    TOW NN12 .... 18 A1
    TOW NN12 .... 19 F1
    TOW NN12 .... 21 J2
    TOW NN12 .... 62 D2
High St North *LBUZ* LU7 .... 77 G5
The High St *CNH/GTH/TM* MK8 .... 35 K5
High Trees *EAG/OLD/WT* MK6 .... 50 A1 🔲
Highveer Cft *EMV/FZ* MK4 .... 60 E2
High Vw *RMKN* MK19 .... 33 K2
Highway *RMKS/WB* MK17 .... 77 F1
Hill Crs *RBEDW* MK43 .... 41 K6
Hillcrest *RBEDW* MK43 .... 29 K3 🔲
Hillcrest Cl *SHEN* MK5 .... 48 E3
Hillcrest Ri *BUCK/WIN* MK18...... 55 H6
Hillersdon Cha
    RMKS/WB MK17 .... 70 C5 🔲
Hillesden Wy *BUCK/WIN* MK18 .... 55 H2 🔲
Hill Farm La *RMKS/WB* MK17...... 66 E3
Hilliard Dr *BDWL* MK13 .... 36 D4
Hills Cl *GTLIN* MK14.................. 25 H6
Hillside Av *TOW* NN12 .... 8 B6
Hillside Rd *LBUZ* LU7 .... 80 B5
Hilltop Av *BUCK/WIN* MK18 ...... 55 H1
Hillview *NPAG* MK16 .... 17 F2
Hillway *RMKS/WB* MK17 .... 52 B3
Hillyer Cf *EAG/OLD/WT* MK6 ...... 38 A6
Himley Gn *LBUZ* LU7 .... 83 J3
Hindemith Gdns
    WTR/OFPK MK7 .... 51 J4 🔲
Hindhead Knoll *WTR/OFPK* MK7.. 51 G3
Hinton Cl *LBUZ* LU7.................. 84 E2
Hinton Ct *BTCHLY* MK3 .... 61 J2
Hoathly Ms *WTR/OFPK* MK7 ...... 51 G1
Hobart Crs *WLLN* MK15 .... 38 A1
Hockliffe Brae *WTR/OFPK* MK7 .... 51 H4
Hockliffe Rd *LBUZ* LU7 .... 84 C2
Hockliffe St *LBUZ* LU7.............. 84 B2 🔲
Hodder La *EMV/FZ* MK4 .... 61 F1

Hodge Lea La *WOLV* MK12 .... 35 K3
Hodgemore Ct *GTLIN* MK14 ...... 25 J3 🔲
Hogarths Ct
    CNH/GTH/TM MK8 .... 36 C6 🔲
Holdom Av *DBGH* MK1................ 62 C1
Holland Wy *NPAG* MK16 .... 26 B2
Holliday Cl *CNH/GTH/TM* MK8 .... 48 B3
The Hollies *LBUZ* LU7 .... 83 K2 🔲
Hollingdon Rd *LBUZ* LU7 .... 78 B4
Hollin La *WOLV* MK12................ 36 B3
Hollinwell Cl *EMV/FZ* MK4.......... 61 G2
Hollister Cha *SHEN* MK5 .... 48 E5
Holloway Dr *BUCK/WIN* MK18 .... 55 H1
Holly Cl *CNH/GTH/TM* MK8 .... 48 B3
Holly Hl *TOW* NN12 .... 4 E5
Holly Wk *RMKS/WB* MK17 .... 64 C1
Holmewood *EMV/FZ* MK4 .... 49 H5
Holmfield Cl *EAG/OLD/WT* MK6 .. 50 C4
Holm Ga *CNH/GTH/TM* MK8 ...... 48 B3
Holst Crs *WTR/OFPK* MK7 .... 51 H5
Holt Gv *SHEN* MK5 .... 48 D1
Holton Hl *EMV/FZ* MK4 .... 61 F1
Holton Rd *BUCK/WIN* MK18........ 55 C1
Holts Gn *RMKS/WB* MK17 .... 71 H4
The Holt *BDWL* MK13 .... 55 H4
Holyhead Crs *EMV/FZ* MK4 .... 61 F3
Holyrood *CNH/GTH/TM* MK8 ...... 48 B1
Holy Thorn La *SHEN* MK5 .... 48 C4
Holywell Pl *EAG/OLD/WT* MK6...... 38 B5
Home Cl *BTCHLY* MK3................ 62 A1
    TOW NN12...................... 4 A1
    TOW NN12 .... 5 F4 🔲
    TOW NN12 .... 18 A1 🔲
Home Farm *RMKS/WB* MK17 ...... 69 G2
Home Farm La
    RMKS/WB MK17 .... 71 J3 🔲
Home Fld *WTR/OFPK* MK7 .... 51 F6
Homeground *BUCK/WIN* MK18 .. 55 H5 🔲
Homestall *BUCK/WIN* MK18 ...... 55 G5
Homestall Cl *SHEN* MK5 .... 48 D2 🔲
The Homestead *SHEN* MK5 ...... 48 D3 🔲
Homestead Wy *TOW* NN12 .... 21 J2
Homeward Ct *SHEN* MK5 .... 48 D2
Honeypot Cl *BDWL* MK13 .... 36 E5 🔲
The Hooke *WLLN* MK15.............. 26 C6
Hooper Ga *WLLN* MK15 .... 26 B6
Hopkins Cl *MKV* MK10.............. 39 F5
Hoppers Meadow *SHEN* MK5 ...... 48 D1
Hornbeam *NPAG* MK16 .... 25 K2
Hornbeam Cl *LBUZ* LU7 .... 84 D1
Hornby Cha *EMV/FZ* MK4 .... 60 E1 🔲
Horn La *STSTR* MK11 .... 34 E2
Horn St *BUCK/WIN* MK18 .... 74 A3
Horsefair Gn *STSTR* MK11.......... 34 E2
Horsepool La *RMKS/WB* MK17.... 53 H6
Horton Ga *GTLIN* MK14 .... 25 J3
Hortonsfield Rd *TOW* NN12 ...... 12 A6
Horwood Ct *DBGH* MK1 .... 62 C2
Hotch Cft *RBEDW* MK43 .... 29 K2 🔲
Houghton Ct
    CNH/GTH/TM MK8 .... 48 C1 🔲
Housman Cl *NPAG* MK16 .... 15 K6
Howard Wy *NPAG* MK16 .... 26 E2
Howe Rock Pl *EMV/FZ* MK4 .... 60 E2
Howland Pl *RMKS/WB* MK17 ...... 65 G4 🔲
Hoylake Cl *BTCHLY* MK3 .... 61 G4
Hubbard Cl *BUCK/WIN* MK18 ...... 55 J2
Huckleberry Cl
    WTR/OFPK MK7 .... 51 G3 🔲
Hudson La *CNH/GTH/TM* MK8 .... 48 A2
Humber Wy *BTCHLY* MK3............ 61 H2
Hunsdon Cl *GTLIN* MK14 .... 37 G1 🔲
Hunstanton Wy *BTCHLY* MK3 ...... 61 G3
Hunt Cl *TOW* NN12.................... 5 F2
Hunter Dr *WEAT* MK2 .... 62 B4
Hunters Reach *BDWL* MK13 ...... 36 D4 🔲
Hunter St *BUCK/WIN* MK18 .... 55 F4
Huntingbrooke
    CNH/GTH/TM MK8 .... 48 C1 🔲
Huntingdon Crs *BTCHLY* MK3 .... 61 F5
Huntsman Gv *GTLIN* MK14 .... 25 K3
Hurley Cft *WTR/OFPK* MK7 .... 39 G6
Hurlstone Gv *EMV/FZ* MK4........ 49 G6
Hutchings Cl *SHEN* MK5 .... 48 D1 🔲
Hutton Av *EAG/OLD/WT* MK6........ 3 G7
Hutton Wy *RMKS/WB* MK17........ 52 C4
Huxley Cl *NPAG* MK16 .... 25 J1
Hyde Cl *NPAG* MK16.................. 26 B3
Hydrus Dr *LBUZ* LU7 .... 84 E1
The Hythe *CNH/GTH/TM* MK8 .... 36 A4

I

Ibstone Av *BDWL* MK13.............. 2 B1
Illingworth Pl
    EAG/OLD/WT MK6 .... 49 J1 🔲

Ingleton Cl *BDWL* MK13 .... 2 A1
Inn Farm Ct *NPAG* MK16 .... 16 C4
Innholder Cl *GTLIN* MK14 .... 37 J1 🔲
Inverness Cl *BTCHLY* MK3 .... 61 J1
Ireland Cl *WTR/OFPK* MK7 .... 51 J5 🔲
Ironmonger Ct *GTLIN* MK14 ...... 37 J1 🔲
Irving Dl *WTR/OFPK* MK7 .... 51 K4
Isaacson Dr *WTR/OFPK* MK7 ..... 51 H2
Islington Br *TOW* NN12 .... 5 F4
Ivy Cl *NPAG* MK16 .... 26 D1
Ivy La *LBUZ* LU7 .... 77 H6
  RMKS/WB MK17 .... 69 F2
  RMKS/WB MK17 .... 71 H6

J

Jacobs Cl *GTLIN* MK14 .... 25 G6
Jamaica *EAG/OLD/WT* MK6 ...... 49 K3 🔲
Jarman Cl *BUCK/WIN* MK18 ...... 55 J3 🔲
Jeeves *EAG/OLD/WT* MK6 .... 50 B2
Jenkins Cl *SHEN* MK5 .... 48 C3
Jenkinson Rd *TOW* NN12 .... 5 G5
Jenna Wy *NPAG* MK16 .... 27 F2
Jennings *GTLIN* MK14 .... 25 F6
Jersey Rd *WOLV* MK12 .... 23 K6
Johnston Pl *EAG/OLD/WT* MK6 .. 49 H1
Jonathans *EAG/OLD/WT* MK6 .... 49 K3
Joules Ct *SHEN* MK5 .... 49 F4
Juniper Cl *TOW* NN12 .... 4 E5
Juniper Gdns *WTR/OFPK* MK7 ... 51 G2
Jupiter Dr *LBUZ* LU7 .... 84 E1

K

Kalman Gdns *WTR/OFPK* MK7 ... 51 J4 🔲
Kaplan Cl *SHEN* MK5 .... 48 E4
Katherine Cl *WTR/OFPK* MK7 .... 51 F5
Katrine Pl *WEAT* MK2 .... 62 C6
Keach Cl *BUCK/WIN* MK18 .... 74 B2
Keasden Ct *EMV/FZ* MK4 .... 60 E1
Keaton Cl *CNH/GTH/TM* MK8 .... 48 A2
Keats Cl *NPAG* MK16 .... 25 K1
Keats Dr *TOW* NN12 .... 4 E4
Keats Wy *BTCHLY* MK3 .... 61 J4
Kellan Dr *EAG/OLD/WT* MK6 ...... 3 J6
Kelso Cl *BTCHLY* MK3 .... 61 G5
Kelvin Dr *SHEN* MK5 .... 49 G3
Kemble Ct *WLLN* MK15 .... 38 A1
Kempton Gdns *BTCHLY* MK3 ..... 61 G5
Kenchester *BDWL* MK13 .... 36 C2
Kendal Gdns *LBUZ* LU7 .... 83 H2
Kenilworth Dr *BTCHLY* MK3 .... 61 H4
Kennel Rd *TOW* NN12 .... 18 E2
Kennels Dr *TOW* NN12 .... 20 B2
Kennet Dr *BTCHLY* MK3 .... 61 H3
Kennington Cl *NPAG* MK16 ..... 26 B2 🔲
Kensington Dr
  CNH/GTH/TM MK8 .... 48 C1
Kents Rd *GTLIN* MK14 .... 25 C5
Kenwell Ct *WLLN* MK15 .... 38 B4 🔲
Kenwood Ga *EAG/OLD/WT* MK6 . 38 A5
Keppel Av *RMKN* MK19 .... 24 A3
Kepwick *CNH/GTH/TM* MK8 .... 36 B6
Kercroft *CNH/GTH/TM* MK8 .... 36 B5
Kerria Pl *BTCHLY* MK3 .... 49 K6
Kersey *GTLIN* MK14 .... 25 F5
Kestrel Wy *BUCK/WIN* MK18 ..... 55 H5
Keswick Dr *RMKN* MK19 .... 13 H1
Ketelbey Nook *WTR/OFPK* MK7 . 51 J4
Ketton Cl *WLLN* MK15 .... 26 C5 🔲
Kew Ct *CNH/GTH/TM* MK8 .... 36 B6
Keyes Wy *BUCK/WIN* MK18 ..... 55 H1 🔲
Keynes Cl *NPAG* MK16 .... 26 D1
Khasiaberry *WTR/OFPK* MK7 .... 51 G4
Kidd Cl *CNH/GTH/TM* MK8 .... 48 B3
Kildonan Pl *WOLV* MK12 .... 36 A3
Kilwinning Dr *MKV* MK10 .... 38 E6
Kimbolton Ct *GTLIN* MK14 ...... 25 K5 🔲
Kincardine Dr *BTCHLY* MK3 ...... 49 H6
Kindermann Ct *SHEN* MK5 ...... 48 E4 🔲
Kindleton *GTLIN* MK14 .... 25 J5
King Charles Cl
  BUCK/WIN MK18 .... 55 H1 🔲
King Edward St *BDWL* MK13 ...... 24 C6
Kingfisher Rd *BUCK/WIN* MK18 . 55 H4
Kingsbridge *EMV/FZ* MK4 .... 61 G1
Kingsfield Piece *TOW* NN12 .... 19 F1
Kingsfold *BDWL* MK13 .... 24 E6
Kings La *TOW* NN12 .... 9 J4
Kingsley Cl *NPAG* MK16 .... 25 J1
Kingsley Rd *TOW* NN12 .... 8 B6
Kingston Br *RMKS/WB* MK17 ..... 39 J5

King St *LBUZ* LU7 .... 84 B1
  STSTR MK11 .... 35 F1
Kinloch Pl *WEAT* MK2 .... 62 C6
Kinnear Cl *CNH/GTH/TM* MK8 ... 48 A2
Kinross Dr *BTCHLY* MK3 .... 61 H1
Kipling Dr *NPAG* MK16 .... 25 J1
  TOW NN12 .... 4 E4
Kipling Rd *BTCHLY* MK3 .... 61 K4
Kirkeby Cl *GTLIN* MK14 .... 37 G1 🔲
Kirke Cl *SHEN* MK5 .... 48 D4
Kirkham St *SHEN* MK5 .... 49 F1
Kirkstall Pl *EAG/OLD/WT* MK6 ... 49 H1
Kirtlington *WLLN* MK15 .... 38 A2
Kiteleys Gn *LBUZ* LU7 .... 84 D1
Knapp Ga *CNH/GTH/TM* MK8 .... 48 C2
Knaves Hl *LBUZ* LU7 .... 83 J1
Knebworth Ga *GTLIN* MK14 .... 25 K4 🔲
Knights Ct *RMKS/WB* MK17 ...... 71 J4
Knoll Cl *NPAG* MK16 .... 16 E1
Knowles Gn *WEAT* MK2 .... 62 B4
Knowl Ga *SHEN* MK5 .... 49 F2
Knox Br *WTR/OFPK* MK7 .... 51 G1
Krohn Cl *BUCK/WIN* MK18 .... 55 J3 🔲
Krypton Cl *SHEN* MK5 .... 49 F4 🔲

L

Laburnum Gv *WEAT* MK2 .... 62 D4
Lacy Dr *WLLN* MK15 .... 38 A1
Ladymead Cl *RMKS/WB* MK17 .. 59 J3 🔲
Lagonda Cl *NPAG* MK16 .... 26 D1
Laidon Cl *WEAT* MK2 .... 62 C6
Lake Cl *BUCK/WIN* MK18 .... 74 C1
Laker Ct *EAG/OLD/WT* MK6 .... 49 H2
Lakes La *NPAG* MK16 .... 16 A6
Lake St *LBUZ* LU7 .... 84 B2 🔲
Lamb Cl *NPAG* MK16 .... 25 K1
Lamberhurst Gv *WTR/OFPK* MK7 51 J1
Lamb La *WTR/OFPK* MK7 .... 51 H2
Lambourn Ct *EMV/FZ* MK4 .... 61 H1
Lambtons Wy
  BUCK/WIN MK18 .... 74 C2 🔲
Lammas *EAG/OLD/WT* MK6 ...... 49 K4
Lammas Wk *LBUZ* LU7 .... 84 B2
Lampitts Cross
  EAG/OLD/WT MK6 .... 50 A3
Lamport Ct *CNH/GTH/TM* MK8 . 48 D1 🔲
Lamva Ct *STSTR* MK11 .... 35 G2 🔲
Lancaster Ga *BTCHLY* MK3 .... 61 H4
Lanchester Rd *RBEDW* MK43 .... 28 E3
Landrace Ct *SHEN* MK5 .... 48 C6 🔲
Landsborough Ga *WLLN* MK15 ... 26 B6
Lanercost Crs *WTR/OFPK* MK7 .. 39 G6
Lane's End *LBUZ* LU7 .... 80 B2
The Lane *RMKS/WB* MK17 .... 76 A1
  TOW NN12 .... 11 J1
Lanfranc Gdns *WLLN* MK15 .... 26 A6
Langcliffe Dr *BDWL* MK13 .... 36 E2
Langdale Cl *WEAT* MK2 .... 70 C1
Langerstone La *EMV/FZ* MK4 .... 60 E2
Langford Pl *WTR/OFPK* MK7 ...... 51 F6
Langland Rd *EAG/OLD/WT* MK6 . 50 B3
Langton Dr *CNH/GTH/TM* MK8 .. 36 B4
Lanthorn Cl *GTLIN* MK14 .... 37 H1 🔲
Larch Gv *WEAT* MK2 .... 62 C4
Lark Cl *BUCK/WIN* MK18 .... 55 H4
Lark La *NPAG* MK16 .... 15 K6
Larkspur Av *GTLIN* MK14 .... 37 H2
Larwood Pl *EAG/OLD/WT* MK6 .... 3 G7
Lasborough Rd *MKV* MK10 .... 39 H6
Lascelles Cl *WLLN* MK15 .... 26 A6 🔲
Laser Cl *SHEN* MK5 .... 49 F3
Lastingham Gv *EMV/FZ* MK4 ... 60 E1 🔲
Latimer *STSTR* MK11 .... 35 F3
Launceston Ct *SHEN* MK5 .... 48 E3 🔲
Launde *WTR/OFPK* MK7 .... 39 G6
Laurel Ct *CNH/GTH/TM* MK8 ..... 48 C2
The Laurels *DBGH* MK1 .... 62 C2 🔲
Lavender Gv *WTR/OFPK* MK7 .... 51 F4
Lawson Pl *SHEN* MK5 .... 48 E4 🔲
Leafield Ri *CNH/GTH/TM* MK8 ... 36 A5
Leapingwell La *BUCK/WIN* MK18 74 C1
Leary Crs *NPAG* MK16 .... 26 D1 🔲
Leasowe Pl *BDWL* MK13 .... 2 A3
Leckhampstead Rd
  BUCK/WIN MK18 .... 44 A2
  RMKN MK19 .... 32 E5
Ledburn Gv *LBUZ* LU7 .... 83 K3
Ledbury *GTLIN* MK14 .... 25 G4
Lees Cl *TOW* NN12 .... 19 F1
Leeson Rd *TOW* NN12 .... 5 F5
Leigh Hl *EMV/FZ* MK4 .... 61 G1
Leighton Rd *LBUZ* LU7 .... 79 F6
  RMKS/WB MK17 .... 70 D6
Leighton St *RMKS/WB* MK17 .... 65 F5
Lenborough Cl *BUCK/WIN* MK18.. 55 F4

Lenborough Ct *WLLN* MK15 ...... 38 B5 🔲
Lenborough Rd *BUCK/WIN* MK18 .. 55 F4
Lennon Dr *CNH/GTH/TM* MK8 ... 48 B2
Lennox Rd *WEAT* MK2 .... 62 C4
Lenthall Cl *BDWL* MK13 .... 36 D2
Leominster Ga *WTR/OFPK* MK7 . 39 F6 🔲
Leonards Lee *EMV/FZ* MK4 .... 60 C1 🔲
Leon Av *WEAT* MK2 .... 62 C3
Leopard Dr *WLLN* MK15 .... 25 K6
Leopold Rd *LBUZ* LU7 .... 83 J2 🔲
Lester Ct *WTR/OFPK* MK7 .... 51 H2
Leven Cl *LBUZ* LU7 .... 83 G2
  WEAT MK2 .... 62 C6
Lewis Cl *NPAG* MK16 .... 15 J6
Leys Cl *SHEN* MK5 .... 48 E1
The Leys *RMKS/WB* MK17 .... 52 C5
Leys Vw *NPAG* MK16 .... 16 E2
Lichfield Down *WTR/OFPK* MK7 . 51 G4
Lightfoot Ct *WTR/OFPK* MK7 ..... 50 E4
Lilac Cl *RMKS/WB* MK17 .... 69 F2 🔲
Lilleshall Av *MKV* MK10 .... 38 E6
Limbaud Cl *WTR/OFPK* MK7 ..... 51 F4
Lime Av *BUCK/WIN* MK18 .... 55 J4
Lime Cl *NPAG* MK16 .... 26 A1
Lime Gv *LBUZ* LU7 .... 83 K1
  RMKS/WB MK17 .... 52 C5
Limerick La *CMK* MK9 .... 38 A4 🔲
Lime Rd *TOW* NN12 .... 11 K5
The Limes *STSTR* MK11 .... 34 E3
  WEAT MK2 .... 62 D3
Linceslade Gv *SHEN* MK5 .... 36 E6
Lincoln *GTLIN* MK14 .... 25 F5
Lincombe Slade *LBUZ* LU7 .... 83 K1
Lincroft *RBEDW* MK43 .... 29 H4
Linden Gv *GTLIN* MK14 .... 25 H5
The Lindens *TOW* NN12 .... 5 G3 🔲
Lindisfarne Dr *MKV* MK10 .... 39 F6
Linford Av *NPAG* MK16 .... 25 K1
Linford La *WLLN* MK15 .... 38 A1
Lingfield *WOLV* MK12 .... 36 B3 🔲
Link Wy *TOW* NN12 .... 5 F4
Linnet Rd *TOW* NN12 .... 5 F6
Linslade Rd *LBUZ* LU7 .... 80 A3
Lintlaw Pl *BTCHLY* MK3 .... 49 K6 🔲
Linton Cl *BDWL* MK13 .... 37 F3
Linwood Gv *LBUZ* LU7 .... 84 C3
The Linx *BTCHLY* MK3 .... 61 K1
Lipscombe Dr
  BUCK/WIN MK18 .... 55 H2 🔲
Lipscomb La *SHEN* MK5 .... 48 D2 🔲
Lissel Rd *EAG/OLD/WT* MK6 ...... 50 D4
Littlecote *CNH/GTH/TM* MK8 ..... 36 D6
Little Habton *EMV/FZ* MK4 .... 60 E1
Little Hame *MKV* MK10 .... 38 E4
Little Horwood Rd
  RMKN MK19 .... 66 D2
Little Linford La *RMKN* MK19 .... 25 H1
Little London *RMKN* MK19 .... 33 J3
  TOW NN12 .... 8 A6
Little Meadow *SHEN* MK5 .... 48 D2
Littlemere *CNH/GTH/TM* MK8 .. 36 A6 🔲
Little Spinney *RBEDW* MK43 ..... 29 K2 🔲
Little Stanton *GTLIN* MK14 ...... 25 G5 🔲
Little Stocking *SHEN* MK5 .... 48 D6
Littleworth *LBUZ* LU7 .... 82 D6
Livesey Hl *SHEN* MK5 .... 48 E4
Livingstone Dr *WLLN* MK15 ...... 38 B2
Llndores Cft *WTR/OFPK* MK7 .... 39 G6
Lloyds *EAG/OLD/WT* MK6 .... 49 K2
Lochy Dr *LBUZ* LU7 .... 83 H2
Locke Rd *WEAT* MK2 .... 62 A3
Lock La *RMKN* MK19 .... 23 F3
Lockton Ct *EMV/FZ* MK4 .... 48 E6
Lock View La *DBGH* MK1 .... 62 D2
Lodge Farm Ct *RMKN* MK19 ...... 13 G5
Lodge Ga *GTLIN* MK14 .... 25 H6 🔲
Lodge La *RMKS/WB* MK17 .... 70 D6
Lodge Pk *RBEDW* MK43 .... 29 H6
Lodge Rd *RBEDW* MK43 .... 29 H6
Lomond Dr *LBUZ* LU7 .... 83 H2
  WEAT MK2 .... 70 B2
London End *RMKS/WB* MK17 .... 65 G5
  RMKS/WB MK17 .... 69 G1
London End La *RMKS/WB* MK17 63 J3
London Rd *BUCK/WIN* MK18 ..... 55 H6
  MKV MK10 .... 39 F2
  NPAG MK16 .... 26 E2
  RMKN MK19 .... 22 D6
  RMKS/WB MK17 .... 65 H6
  SHEN MK5 .... 48 D2
  STSTR MK11 .... 34 E2
  TOW NN12 .... 5 H5
Long Ayres *WTR/OFPK* MK7 ...... 51 F6
Longbournes *RBEDW* MK43 ..... 29 K3 🔲
Longcroft La *TOW* NN12 .... 10 B3
Longcross *WLLN* MK15 .... 37 K1
Longfellow Dr *NPAG* MK16 .... 25 K1 🔲
Longhedge *WTR/OFPK* MK7 ...... 63 F1 🔲

Longlands Ct *BUCK/WIN* MK18 . 55 F4
Longleat Ct *CNH/GTH/TM* MK8 ..
Longpeak Cl *EMV/FZ* MK4 ....
Longville *WOLV* MK12 ....
Lords Cl *WEAT* MK2 ....
Lordsmead *RBEDW* MK43 ....
Loriner Pl *GTLIN* MK14 ....
Loseley Ct *CNH/GTH/TM* MK8 ...
Lothersdale *BDWL* MK13 ....
Lothian Cl *BTCHLY* MK3 ....
Loughton Rd *BDWL* MK13 ....
Lovat St *NPAG* MK16 ....
Lovatt Dr *BTCHLY* MK3 ....
Lovent Dr *LBUZ* LU7 ....
Lower Eighth St *CMK* MK9 ....
Lower End *BUCK/WIN* MK18 ......
Lower End Rd *RMKS/WB* MK17 ..
Lower Fourth St *CMK* MK9 ....
Lower Ninth St *CMK* MK9 ....
Lower Second St *CMK* MK9 ....
Lower Stable Yd *TOW* NN12 ......
Lower Stonehayes *GTLIN* MK14 .
Lower St *TOW* NN12 ....
Lower Tenth St *CMK* MK9 ....
Lower Third St *CMK* MK9 ....
Lower Wy *RMKS/WB* MK17 ....
Lowland Rd *EMV/FZ* MK4 ....
Lowndes Wy *BUCK/WIN* MK18...
Lownes Gv *SHEN* MK5 ....
Loxbeare Dr *EMV/FZ* MK4 ....
Loyne Cl *LBUZ* LU7 ....
Lucas Pl *EAG/OLD/WT* MK6 ......
Luccombe *EMV/FZ* MK4 ....
Lucy La *SHEN* MK5 ....
Ludgate *EAG/OLD/WT* MK6 ....
Ludlow Cl *BTCHLY* MK3 ....
Lufford Pk *GTLIN* MK14 ....
Lullingston Dr *BDWL* MK13 ....
Lumber La *TOW* NN12 ....
Lundholme *BDWL* MK13 ....
Lutyens Gv *WTR/OFPK* MK7 ......
Lydiard *CNH/GTH/TM* MK8 ....
Lynmouth Crs *EMV/FZ* MK4 ......
Lynott Cl *CNH/GTH/TM* MK8.......
Lyon Rd *DBGH* MK1 ....
Lyra Gdns *LBUZ* LU7 ....
Lywood Rd *LBUZ* LU7 ....

M

Maclaren Ct *EAG/OLD/WT* MK6 .
Magdalen Cl *STSTR* MK11 ....
Magenta Cl *WEAT* MK2 ....
Magpie Cl *SHEN* MK5 ....
Magpie Rd *TOW* NN12 ....
Magpie Wy *BUCK/WIN* MK18 .....
Mahler Cl *WTR/OFPK* MK7 ....
Maidenhead Av *BDWL* MK13 .....
Maidstone Rd *MKV* MK10 ....
Main Dr *TOW* NN12 ....
Main Rd *RMKS/WB* MK17 ....
  TOW NN12 ....
Main St *BUCK/WIN* MK18 ....
  RMKN MK19 ....
  RMKN MK19 ....
  RMKS/WB MK17 ....
Malins Ga *GTLIN* MK14 ....
Mallard Dr *BUCK/WIN* MK18 ......
Malletts Cl *STSTR* MK11 ....
Mallow Ga *GTLIN* MK14 ....
Maltings Cl *RBEDW* MK43 ....
The Maltings *BUCK/WIN* MK18...
  LBUZ LU7 ....
Malvern Dr *LBUZ* LU7 ....
  STSTR MK11 ....
Mandeville Dr *MKV* MK10 ....
Manifold La *SHEN* MK5 ....
Manor Cl *MKV* MK10 ....
  RMKN MK19 ....
  RMKN MK19 ....
  RMKS/WB MK17 ....
Manor Dr *RMKN* MK19 ....
Manorfields Rd *RMKN* MK19 ......
Manor Pk *BUCK/WIN* MK18 ....
Manor Rd *BUCK/WIN* MK18 ....
  NPAG MK16 ....
  RMKS/WB MK17 ....
  WEAT MK2 ....
  WOLV MK12 ....
Manor St *BUCK/WIN* MK18 ....
Manor Wy *TOW* NN12 ....
Manse Cl *STSTR* MK11 ....
Mansel Cl *RMKN* MK19 ....
Mansell Cl *SHEN* MK5 ....
Manshead Ct *STSTR* MK11 ....
Maple Cl *TOW* NN12 ....

ean WOLV MK12 .... 36 B2
urham WTR/OFPK MK7 .. 51 G6 3
v RMKS/WB MK17 .... 52 B5
MK2 .... 62 D3
Vy RBEDW MK43 .... 29 H5
Meadow RMKS/WB MK17 .. 51 J2
Rd LBUZ LU7 .... 84 A3
l LBUZ LU7........................... 83 H2
ys BUCK/WIN MK18 .... 55 J3
d Pl GTLIN MK14 .... 37 H3
Dr WOLV MK12 .... 36 A2
m Pl GTLIN MK14 .... 37 H3
Hl BUCK/WIN MK18 .... 55 G2
Sq BUCK/WIN MK18 .... 55 G2 1
LU7 .... 84 B2 4
MK19 .... 13 H1 1
ough Ga CMK MK9................ 3 H2
ough St CMK MK9 .... 3 H2
LD/WT MK6........................... 50 C4
MK14 .... 25 F5
ields LBUZ LU7 .... 84 E3
Gv CNH/GTH/TM MK8........... 48 B2
Dr NPAG MK16 .... 25 K1
Rd TOW NN12 .... 5 G4
Ct RMKS/WB MK17 .... 65 G4
Cl EAG/OLD/WT MK6........... 49 K4
La WOLV MK12 .... 35 K2
s La WLLN MK15 .... 38 B5
v Pl EMV/FZ MK4 .... 61 F1 5
r GTLIN MK14 .... 25 H3
nd Rd NPAG MK16 .... 26 B1
orth EAG/OLD/WT MK6...... 50 C3
l BUCK/WIN MK18 .... 55 J4
MK14 .... 37 H1
ale Pl GTLIN MK14 .... 37 J2 2
kins Dr LBUZ LU7 .... 84 A1 3
d Cl EMV/FZ MK4 .... 49 G6 5
d Rd WLLN MK15 .... 26 A5
acmanus Dr
WIN MK18 .... 55 G2
d Cl NPAG MK16 .... 25 K1 3
d Gv BTCHLY MK3 .... 61 K4
r EAG/OLD/WT MK6 .... 50 A4
TLIN MK14 .... 25 F5
l WLLN MK15 .... 38 A1
en Rd BDWL MK13................ 36 D1
Gdns SHEN MK5.................... 48 E3
v Ct SHEN MK5 .... 48 E3 3
y Cl SHEN MK5...................... 48 E3
Gdns GTLIN MK14 .... 25 K5
liff Dr EMV/FZ MK4 .... 60 D3
SHEN MK5 .... 48 D6 2
n Pl BDWL MK13 .... 2 A2
dns SHEN MK5....................... 49 F4
d Cl BDWL MK13 .... 36 D4 3
y TOW NN12 .... 21 J2
ell Dr WOLV MK12 .... 24 A6
e Cl BUCK/WIN MK18 ..... 55 G3 2
Gdns BUCK/WIN MK18 ..... 55 H5
La MKV MK10 .... 39 F4
sweet
OFPK MK7 .... 51 G4 2
Vw RMKS/WB MK17 .... 52 E3
N12 .... 21 J2
Wy LBUZ LU7 .... 82 D6
LU7 .... 84 E2
BDWL MK13 .... 24 D5
d LBUZ LU7............................ 78 D4
y BUCK/WIN MK18 .... 55 G5
LU7 .... 84 D1
dway SHEN MK5.................... 48 D1
Rd EAG/OLD/WT MK6 .... 49 K4
ell EMV/FZ MK4 .... 49 H6 2
st CNH/GTH/TM MK8 ..... 36 B5 1
EAG/OLD/WT MK6 .... 50 C2
Cl NPAG MK16 .... 26 D2 3
La TOW NN12 .... 5 F3
Oak La BUCK/WIN MK18 .. 74 C2
Dr LBUZ LU7 .... 83 G2
MK2 .... 70 C1
d EAG/OLD/WT MK6 .... 49 K5
Av BTCHLY MK3 .... 49 K6
GTLIN MK14 .... 25 F5
sohn Gv WTR/OFPK MK7 .. 51 H5
re Ct
TH/TM MK8 .... 48 C1 7
re Gdns LBUZ LU7 .... 83 K4
re Rd LBUZ LU7 .... 83 K4
e Av RMKS/WB MK17........... 52 E5
Ct SHEN MK5.......................... 48 E5
Dr BDWL MK13 .... 36 E1
nt La RBEDW MK43 .... 29 G3
Gv CNH/GTH/TM MK8 .... 48 B2
Wy LBUZ LU7 .... 84 E1
ood Dr SHEN MK5.................. 48 B5
Cl BTCHLY MK3 .... 61 H2
Wy BTCHLY MK3...................... 61 H2
Gv EMV/FZ MK4 .... 60 E3

Merton Dr EAG/OLD/WT MK6.......... 49 K5
Metcalfe Gv GTLIN MK14................. 26 A3
Michigan Dr WLLN MK15.................. 26 B5
Mickleton WLLN MK15 .... 37 K1
Middlefield Cl
BUCK/WIN MK18 .... 55 H2 4
Middle Gn LBUZ LU7 .... 84 D1
Middlesex Dr BTCHLY MK3 .... 61 J2
Middle Slade BUCK/WIN MK18........ 55 G5
Middleton GTLIN MK14 .... 25 H6
Midshires Wy BDWL MK13 .... 36 C2
CNH/GTH/TM MK8 .... 48 B4
RMKN MK19.. 14 C5
RMKS/WB MK17 .... 58 B5
RMKS/WB MK17 .... 67 K2
Midsummer Bvd CMK MK9 .... 2 C6
Midway LBUZ LU7 .... 84 D2
Mikern Cl WEAT MK2 .... 62 B3
Milburn Av EAG/OLD/WT MK6 .... 49 H1
Milebush LBUZ LU7 .... 83 H1
Milecastle BDWL MK13 .... 36 D2
Miles Av LBUZ LU7 .... 84 C1
Miles Cl GTLIN MK14.......................... 25 K2
Milesmere CNH/GTH/TM MK8 .... 36 A6
Miletree Ct LBUZ LU7 .... 84 C1
Mile Tree Rd LBUZ LU7 .... 80 E4
Milfoil Av GTLIN MK14 .... 37 G3
Milford Av STSTR MK11...................... 35 F3
Millards Cl RBEDW MK43.................... 29 K3
Millbank LBUZ LU7.............................. 84 A1
Millbank Pl WTR/OFPK MK7 .... 51 G1
Mill Ct WOLV MK12 .... 35 H2
Millers Cl LBUZ LU7 .... 84 E2 2
Millers Wy STSTR MK11 .... 35 H4
WOLV MK12 .... 36 B2
Millfield Cl RBEDW MK43 .... 29 J3
Millhayes GTLIN MK14 .... 25 J5
Millholm Ri EAG/OLD/WT MK6......... 50 D4
Millington Ga WLLN MK15 .... 26 C5
Mill La BDWL MK13.............................. 24 D6
BUCK/WIN MK18 .... 55 F3
RMKS/WB MK17 .... 40 D4
RMKS/WB MK17 .... 52 C4
RMKS/WB MK17 .... 70 D3
STSTR MK11 .... 34 D2
TOW NN12 .... 4 B2
WLLN MK15 .... 38 B4
Mill Rd LBUZ LU7 .... 84 B1
LBUZ LU7 .... 85 K2
RBEDW MK43.. 29 J3
WEAT MK2 .... 62 D4
Mill Sq WOLV MK12.............................. 35 H2
Millstream Wy LBUZ LU7 .... 84 A2
Mill St NPAG MK16 .... 16 C6
Mill Wy RMKS/WB MK17 .... 52 E4
Milton Dr NPAG MK16 .... 26 D1
Milton Gv BTCHLY MK3 .... 61 J5
Milton Keynes Boundary Wk
EMV/FZ MK4 .... 60 B4
RMKN MK19... 47 G3
RMKS/WB MK17 .... 40 D2
RMKS/WB MK17 .... 47 H5
RMKS/WB MK17 .... 52 B2
RMKS/WB MK17 .... 64 A2
RNHPTN NN7.. 12 B1
Milton Rd WLLN MK15......................... 26 C6
WTR/OFPK MK7.................................... 50 E2
Minerva Gdns WTR/OFPK MK7 .... 51 H2
Minshull Cl BUCK/WIN MK18 .... 55 G2 2
Minstrel Ct BDWL MK13 .... 24 E6
Minton Cl GTLIN MK14......................... 25 K4
Missenden Cl BUCK/WIN MK18 .. 74 A3 2
Mitcham Pl BDWL MK13 .... 2 C3
Mitchell Rd RBEDW MK43................... 29 F3
Mithras Gdns WTR/OFPK MK7 .... 51 H3
Mitre St BUCK/WIN MK18 .... 55 F4
Moat La TOW NN12 .... 5 F3
Moeran Cl WTR/OFPK MK7................. 51 H4
Monellan Gv WTR/OFPK MK7............ 51 F6
Monks Wy BDWL MK13......................... 36 B3
CNH/GTH/TM MK8 .... 35 K5
GTLIN MK14 .... 25 K5
WLLN MK15 .... 26 A4
Monro Av CNH/GTH/TM MK8............ 48 B2
Montagu Dr EAG/OLD/WT MK6 .... 50 A1
Montgomery Cl LBUZ LU7 .... 80 C6
Montgomery Crs WLLN MK15 .... 25 K6
Moon St WOLV MK12 .... 36 A1
Moorend Rd TOW NN12 .... 11 K5
Moorfield RMKS/WB MK17.................. 69 G2
Moorfoot STSTR MK11 .... 35 H3
Moorgate EAG/OLD/WT MK6 .... 49 J2
Moorhen Wy BUCK/WIN MK18 .... 55 H3
Moorhills Crs LBUZ LU7...................... 82 D6
Moorlands LBUZ LU7............................ 82 D6
Moorlands Rd LBUZ LU7..................... 82 E6
Moor Pk BTCHLY MK3 .... 61 G3
Morar Cl LBUZ LU7................................ 83 H2

Mordaunts Ct WLLN MK15 .... 38 B5 5
Morebath Gv EMV/FZ MK4.............. 49 F5
Moreton Dr BUCK/WIN MK18.......... 43 H6
Moreton Rd BUCK/WIN MK18 .... 55 G1
Morley Crs WTR/OFPK MK7 .... 51 H5
Morrell Cl SHEN MK5 .... 48 E4 3
Morrison Ct CNH/GTH/TM MK8 ...... 48 B3
Mortain Cl WTR/OFPK MK7............... 51 G6
Mortons Fk BDWL MK13..................... 36 C1
Mossdale BDWL MK13 .... 36 E2 1
Mount Av DBGH MK1............................ 50 C6
Mountbatten Gdns LBUZ LU7 .... 80 C6 1
Mounthill Av RMKN MK19................. 22 C6
Mount Pleasant
EAG/OLD/WT MK6............................... 50 D5
LBUZ LU7 .... 78 D4 2
RMKS/WB MK17 .... 53 G5
RMKS/WB MK17 .... 70 D6
TOW NN12 .... 12 A5
Mount Pleasant Cl
BUCK/WIN MK18 .... 55 F4
Mountsfield Cl NPAG MK16 .... 26 B2
The Mount EAG/OLD/WT MK6 .... 50 D5
RMKS/WB MK17 .... 52 E5
Mowbray Dr LBUZ LU7 .... 83 J2
Mozart Cl WTR/OFPK MK7 .... 51 H5
Muddiford La EMV/FZ MK4 .... 49 G6
Muirfield Dr BTCHLY MK3 .... 61 G3
Mullen Av GTLIN MK14 .... 37 J2 3
Mullion Pl EAG/OLD/WT MK6 .... 3 J6
Murrey Cl SHEN MK5 .... 49 F4 2
Mursley Ct STSTR MK11 .... 35 G2
Mursley Rd RMKS/WB MK17 .... 67 F3
Murswell Cl TOW NN12....................... 18 A1
Murswell La TOW NN12 .... 18 A1
Myrtle Bank WOLV MK12 .... 36 A2

N

Nairn Ct BTCHLY MK3 .... 61 H1
Naisby Dr RMKS/WB MK17................ 71 H4
Naphill Pl BDWL MK13............................ 2 B2
Napier St WEAT MK2 .... 62 C3
Narrow Pth RMKS/WB MK17 .... 52 C6
Naseby Cl NPAG MK16........................ 25 K2
Naseby Ct BDWL MK13 .... 36 E1 3
BUCK/WIN MK18 .... 55 H1 9
Nash Cft EMV/FZ MK4.......................... 60 E3
Nash Rd BUCK/WIN MK18.................. 57 G3
RMKS/WB MK17 .... 59 H2
RMKS/WB MK17 .... 66 B1
Nathanial Cl SHEN MK5 .... 48 E4 4
Neapland EAG/OLD/WT MK6 .... 50 A4
Neath Crs BTCHLY MK3 .... 61 K1
Nebular Ct LBUZ LU7 .... 84 D1
Nelson Cl CNH/GTH/TM MK8 .... 48 B3
Nelson Rd LBUZ LU7 .... 80 C6
Nelson St BUCK/WIN MK18................ 55 F3
Nene Cl NPAG MK16............................ 26 C2
Nene Dr BTCHLY MK3 .... 61 H3
Nene La TOW NN12 .... 4 D3
Neptune Gdns LBUZ LU7 .... 84 E1 2
Ness Wy WEAT MK2 .... 62 C6
Nether Gv SHEN MK5 .... 48 D6
Nettlecombe EMV/FZ MK4 .... 49 F6 2
Nevill Cl RMKN MK19............................ 13 J1
Nevis Cl LBUZ LU7 .... 83 H2
Nevis Gv WEAT MK2............................. 62 D6
Newark Ct WTR/OFPK MK7 .... 51 F6 2
Newbolt Cl NPAG MK16........................ 15 J6
TOW NN12 .... 10 A3 1
Newbridge Ov EMV/FZ MK4 .... 48 E6
Newbury Ct BTCHLY MK3 .... 61 G5
Newby Pl EMV/FZ MK4......................... 60 E1
New College Ct BUCK/WIN MK18 .. 42 E5
Newlyn Pl EAG/OLD/WT MK6............... 3 K5
Newman Wy LBUZ LU7 .... 84 C2 1
Newmarket Ct MKV MK10 .... 39 H5
Newport Rd BDWL MK13 .... 24 B6
EAG/OLD/WT MK6................................. 50 C3
NPAG MK16 .... 17 J2
RMKN MK19.. 13 J1
RMKS/WB MK17 .... 51 J1
WLLN MK15 .... 26 C6
New Rd LBUZ LU7 .... 83 K2
RMKN MK19.. 13 G6
RMKS/WB MK17 .... 77 F2
TOW NN12 .... 4 A1
New St STSTR MK11 .... 34 E2
Newton Rd BTCHLY MK3....................... 61 H5
RMKS/WB MK17 .... 69 G5
Nicholas Md GTLIN MK14 .... 25 J5
Nightingale Crs BDWL MK13 .... 24 C6
Nightingale Dr TOW NN12 .... 5 F6
Nightingale Pl
BUCK/WIN MK18 .... 55 H2 5

Nixons Cl EAG/OLD/WT MK6........... 49 H3
Noble Cl WLLN MK15 .... 25 K6 4
Noon Layer Dr MKV MK10 .... 38 D4
Norbrek CNH/GTH/TM MK8 .... 36 B5
Normandy Wy BTCHLY MK3............. 61 H1
Norrington CNH/GTH/TM MK8 .. 36 B5 2
Northampton Rd NPAG MK16 .... 16 C4
RMKN MK19... 22 D4
TOW NN12 .... 5 F2
North Buckinghamshire Wy
RMKS/WB MK17 .... 58 B5
STSTR MK11 .... 35 J5
WOLV MK12 .... 23 J6
North Cl RMKS/WB MK17 .... 77 F2
Northcourt LBUZ LU7 .... 80 B6
North Crawley Rd NPAG MK16 ...... 17 K6
North Cft BUCK/WIN MK18............... 74 B3
Northcroft SHEN MK5......................... 48 E3
North Eighth St CMK MK9 .... 2 E3
North Eleventh St CMK MK9 .... 3 F2
Northend Sq BUCK/WIN MK18 .. 55 G2 3
Northfield Dr WLLN MK15 .... 38 E2
North Fifth St CMK MK9 .... 2 C4
North Fourteenth St CMK MK9......... 3 G1
North Fourth St CMK MK9 .... 2 B5
Northgate TOW NN12............................ 4 E2
North Grafton BDWL MK13 .... 2 A5
Northleigh EMV/FZ MK4..................... 61 G1
North Ninth St CMK MK9 .... 2 E3
North Rdg EAG/OLD/WT MK6 .... 38 A6 2
North Rw CMK MK9............................... 2 A5
North Saxon GTLIN MK14 .... 2 D3
North Secklow GTLIN MK14 .... 2 E1
North Second St CMK MK9.................. 2 B5
North Seventh St CMK MK9 .... 2 D3
North Sixth St CMK MK9....................... 2 D4
North Sq NPAG MK16.......................... 16 C6
North Star Dr LBUZ LU7 .... 84 D1
North St BDWL MK13 .... 24 D6 3
LBUZ LU7 .... 84 B2
RMKN MK19... 13 H6
WEAT MK2 .... 62 B2
North Tenth St CMK MK9 .... 2 E2
North Third St CMK MK9..................... 2 B5
North Thirteenth St CMK MK9........... 3 G1
North Twelfth St CMK MK9 .... 3 F2
North Wy RMKN MK19 .... 33 K2
TOW NN12 .... 21 K3
Northwich EAG/OLD/WT MK6 .... 50 C2
North Witan BDWL MK13 .... 2 C4
Norton Crs TOW NN12 .... 4 E3
Norton Leys WTR/OFPK MK7 .... 51 H2
The Nortons WTR/OFPK MK7............ 51 G6
Norwood La NPAG MK16 .... 26 B2
Nova Ldg EMV/FZ MK4 .... 60 E1
Novello Cft WTR/OFPK MK7............... 51 J5
Nursery Gdns BDWL MK13 .... 36 D3
Nutmeg Cl WTR/OFPK MK7 .... 51 G4 3

O

Oak Bank Dr LBUZ LU7 .... 80 B4
Oak Cl TOW NN12.................................... 5 F5
Oakhill Cl SHEN MK5 .... 48 B3
Oakhill Rd SHEN MK5 .... 48 C3
Oakley Gdns GTLIN MK14 .... 37 K2
Oakley Gn LBUZ LU7 .... 80 C6
Oakridge EMV/FZ MK4 .... 49 H5
Oak Wy BUCK/WIN MK18 .... 74 B3
Oakwood Dr WEAT MK2 .... 62 D4
Oatfield Gdns LBUZ LU7 .... 84 E2 3
Oat Hill Rd TOW NN12............................ 5 F5
Octavian Dr BDWL MK13 .... 36 C2
Odell Cl EAG/OLD/WT MK6 .... 50 B1 1
Offas La BUCK/WIN MK18.................... 74 C2
Old Belle Cl RMKS/WB MK17 .... 70 D6
Oldbrook Bvd EAG/OLD/WT MK6 .. 49 J1
Old Chapel Ms LBUZ LU7 .... 84 B3 3
Olde Bell La SHEN MK5 .... 48 D2
Old English Cl RMKS/WB MK17 .. 58 D2 1
Old Greens Norton Roa
TOW NN12 .... 4 E2
Old Groveway EAG/OLD/WT MK6 .. 50 C4
Old Linslade Rd LBUZ LU7 .... 79 J5
Old Manor Cl RMKS/WB MK17 .... 59 J2
Old Mill Furlong BUCK/WIN MK18 .. 74 B2
Old Oak Dr TOW NN12.......................... 18 A1
Old Rd LBUZ LU7 .... 83 K2
Old Tan Yard Cl
BUCK/WIN MK18 .... 74 A3 3
Old Tiffield Rd TOW NN12 .... 4 E2
Old Wolverton Rd WOLV MK12 .... 23 K5
Oliver Rd WEAT MK2 .... 62 B3
Omega Ct LBUZ LU7 .... 84 D1 2
Onslow Ct WTR/OFPK MK7.................. 51 F5
Orbison Ct CNH/GTH/TM MK8 .... 48 A1

Orchard Cl *BTCHLY* MK3 .... 61 J4
  RBEDW MK43 .... 29 H4 🔢
  RMKS/WB MK17 .... 69 F2 🔢
  TOW NN12 .... 5 F5
  TOW NN12 .... 12 A5
Orchard Dr *LBUZ* LU7 .... 83 J3
Orchard Est *LBUZ* LU7 .... 85 H2
The Orchard *TOW* NN12 .... 21 H2
Orchard Wy *RBEDW* MK43 .... 29 H4
Orford Cl *SHEN* MK5 .... 48 D3 🔢
Orion Wy *LBUZ* LU7 .... 84 E1
Orkney Cl *BTCHLY* MK3 .... 61 J1 🔢
Ormonde *GTLIN* MK14 .... 25 G6
Ormsgill Cl *BDWL* MK13 .... 36 E2
Orne Gdns *WLLN* MK15 .... 38 C1
Orpington Gv *SHEN* MK5 .... 48 E5 🔢
Ortensia Dr *WTR/OFPK* MK7 ..... 51 H2
Orwell Cl *NPAG* MK16 .... 15 J6
Osborne St *WEAT* MK2 .... 62 B4
Osbourne St *WOLV* MK12 .... 36 A1
Osier La *SHEN* MK5 .... 48 E5
Osprey Cl *EAG/OLD/WT* MK6 ..... 49 K1
Osprey Wk *BUCK/WIN* MK18 ..... 55 U3 🔢
Ostlers La *STSTR* MK11 .... 34 E1
Otter Cl *BTCHLY* MK3 .... 61 G2
Otters Brook *BUCK/WIN* MK18 ... 55 H4
Ouse La *TOW* NN12 .... 4 D3
Ousebank Wy *NPAG* MK16 .... 16 C6
Ousebank Wy *STSTR* MK11 .... 34 E2
Ouzel Cl *BTCHLY* MK3 .... 61 H2
The Oval *EAG/OLD/WT* MK6 ...... 49 H2
Overend Cl *BDWL* MK13 .... 36 D3
Overend Green La *LBUZ* LU7 ..... 80 D1
Overgate *CMK* MK9 .... 38 A3
  GTLIN MK14 .... 38 A2
Overn Av *BUCK/WIN* MK18 .... 55 G2
Overn Cl *BUCK/WIN* MK18 .... 55 G2
Overn Crs *BUCK/WIN* MK18 .... 55 F2
Oversley Ct *GTLIN* MK14 .... 25 K4 🔢
Overstreet *GTLIN* MK14 .... 25 J6
Oville Ct *SHEN* MK5 .... 48 D4
Ovitts Cl *BUCK/WIN* MK18 .... 74 B2
Oxendon Ct *LBUZ* LU7 .... 80 A5
Oxford St *WEAT* MK2 .... 62 B3
  WOLV MK12 .... 36 A1
Oxman La *WOLV* MK12 .... 35 H2
Oxwich Gv *EMV/FZ* MK4 .... 60 E3

P

The Paddocks *LBUZ* LU7 .... 83 K2
  TOW NN12 .... 6 C1
Paddock Wy *WEAT* MK2 .... 62 C2
Padstow Av *EAG/OLD/WT* MK6 ..... 3 H6
Page Hill Av *BUCK/WIN* MK18 ... 55 H2
Palace Sq *EAG/OLD/WT* MK6 ..... 49 J2
Palladian Br *BUCK/WIN* MK18 ... 42 D2
Palmers Moor *BUCK/WIN* MK18 ... 57 F3
Pannier Pl *GTLIN* MK14 .... 37 K2
Paprika Ct *WTR/OFPK* MK7 ...... 51 G4 🔢
Paradise *NPAG* MK16 .... 26 A1
Park Av *NPAG* MK16 .... 26 A1
Park Cl *RMKN* MK19 .... 23 F3
  TOW NN12 .... 19 F1
Parker Cl *BDWL* MK13 .... 36 D1
Park Gdns *BTCHLY* MK3 .... 61 K2
Parklands *GTLIN* MK14 .... 25 G4
Park La *TOW* NN12 .... 10 A4
Park Ms *TOW* NN12 .... 5 F3
Park Rd *BUCK/WIN* MK18 .... 74 A2
  NPAG MK16 .... 17 F1
  RMKN MK19 .... 13 J1
  STSTR MK11 .... 34 E2
Park Rd South *BUCK/WIN* MK18 ... 74 A3
Parkside *EMV/FZ* MK4 .... 49 H6
Park St *RMKS/WB* MK17 .... 65 G4
  TOW NN12 .... 5 F3
Park View Rd *TOW* NN12 .... 5 G4
Parkway *RMKS/WB* MK17 .... 52 B3
  RMKS/WB MK17 .... 63 J1
Parnleys *MKV* MK10 .... 38 E5
Parsley Cl *WTR/OFPK* MK7 ...... 51 G4
Parson Cl *BUCK/WIN* MK18 .... 74 A3
Parsons Crs *SHEN* MK5 .... 49 F4
Partridge Cl *BUCK/WIN* MK18 ... 55 J4 🔢
Partridge Piece *RBEDW* MK43 ... 29 K2
Passalewe La *WTR/OFPK* MK7 ... 51 H2
Passmore *EAG/OLD/WT* MK6 ..... 50 B3
  WTR/OFPK MK7 .... 51 F6 🔢
Pastern Pl *GTLIN* MK14 .... 37 K2
Patricks La *RMKN* MK19 .... 33 K3
Patriot Dr *BDWL* MK13 .... 36 E5
Pattison La *WLLN* MK15 .... 38 B4
Paxton Crs *SHEN* MK5 .... 48 E4
Paynes Dr *SHEN* MK5 .... 48 D1
Peacock Hay *EMV/FZ* MK4 ...... 61 F1 🔢

Pearse Gv *WTR/OFPK* MK7 .... 51 F5
Pear Tree La *LBUZ* LU7 .... 84 B1
Peckover Ct
  CNH/GTH/TM MK8 .... 36 C6 🔢
Peebles Pl *BTCHLY* MK3 .... 49 J6
Peel Rd *WOLV* MK12 .... 35 K1
Peers Dr *RMKS/WB* MK17 .... 53 F6
Peers La *SHEN* MK5 .... 48 E3
Pegasus Rd *LBUZ* LU7 .... 84 D1
Pelham Pl *GTLIN* MK14 .... 37 J2 🔢
Pelton Ct *SHEN* MK5 .... 48 E3
Pencarrow Pl *EAG/OLD/WT* MK6.... 3 J7
Pengelly Ct *EAG/OLD/WT* MK6 ..... 3 J7
Penhale Cl *EMV/FZ* MK4 .... 60 E3
Penina Cl *BTCHLY* MK3 .... 61 G2
Penlee Ri *EMV/FZ* MK4 .... 60 E3
Penley Wy *LBUZ* LU7 .... 84 B4
Penmon Cl *MKV* MK10 .... 38 E6 🔢
Pennivale Cl *LBUZ* LU7 .... 84 B1
Penn Rd *WEAT* MK2 .... 62 D3
Pennycress Wy *NPAG* MK16 ...... 25 J1
Pennyroyal *WTR/OFPK* MK7 ..... 51 G2
Penryn Av *EAG/OLD/WT* MK6...... 3 J6
Pentewan Ga *EAG/OLD/WT* MK6.... 3 H6
Pentlands *GTLIN* MK14 .... 35 G3
Percheron Pl *GTLIN* MK14.......... 37 J2
Peregrine Ct *EAG/OLD/WT* MK6 .. 50 A1
Permayne *BDWL* MK13 .... 24 C6
Perracombe *EMV/FZ* MK4 .... 49 H6
Perran Av *EAG/OLD/WT* MK6 ...... 3 J7
Perth Cl *BTCHLY* MK3 .... 61 J1
Peterborough Ga *WLLN* MK15 .... 38 B1 🔢
Petersham Cl *NPAG* MK16 .... 26 B3 🔢
Pettingrew Cl *WTR/OFPK* MK7 ... 51 G3
Petworth *CNH/GTH/TM* MK8 ..... 36 B6
Pevensey Cl *BTCHLY* MK3 .... 61 H4
Peverel Dr *DBGH* MK1 .... 50 A6
Phillimore Cl *WLLN* MK15 .... 26 A6 🔢
Phillip Ct *SHEN* MK5 .... 48 E3
Phoebe La *RMKS/WB* MK17 .... 51 K2
Phoebe's Orch *RMKS/WB* MK17 ... 70 D6
Phoenix Cl *LBUZ* LU7 .... 80 E6
Phoenix Dr *EAG/OLD/WT* MK6 ... 49 H3
Pickering Dr *EMV/FZ* MK4 .... 60 E1
Pightle Crs *BUCK/WIN* MK18 ..... 55 G1
The Pightle *BUCK/WIN* MK18 .... 43 H5
Pigott Dr *SHEN* MK5 .... 48 D4
Pilch La *RMKS/WB* MK17 .... 57 H6
Pilgrim St *GTLIN* MK14.............. 37 K3
Pimpernel Gv *WTR/OFPK* MK7 ... 51 G3
Pine Cl *LBUZ* LU7 .... 80 B5
Pine Gv *RMKS/WB* MK17 .... 52 B5
Pinewood Dr *WEAT* MK2 .... 62 C4
Pinfold *WTR/OFPK* MK7 .... 51 G3
Pinkard Ct *EAG/OLD/WT* MK6 ... 50 B1
Pinkle Hill Rd *LBUZ* LU7 .... 80 B2
Pinkworthy *EMV/FZ* MK4 .... 49 G5
Pipard *GTLIN* MK14 .... 25 H6
Pipston Gn *WTR/OFPK* MK7 ...... 51 G2
Pitcher La *SHEN* MK5 .... 48 E1
Pitchford Av *BUCK/WIN* MK18 ... 55 H1
Pitfield *STSTR* MK11 .... 35 J4
Pitt Gn *BUCK/WIN* MK18 .... 55 J3
Plank Houses *TOW* NN12 .... 7 J4
Plantain Ct *WTR/OFPK* MK7 ..... 51 G3 🔢
Plantation Rd *LBUZ* LU7 .... 80 A3
Pleshey Cl *SHEN* MK5 .... 48 E3 🔢
Plessey Cl *TOW* NN12 .... 5 G4
Plough Cl *RBEDW* MK43 .... 29 H5
Plover Cl *BUCK/WIN* MK18 .... 55 H5
  NPAG MK16 .... 26 E2
  TOW NN12 .... 5 F6 🔢
Plowman Cl *WOLV* MK12 .... 35 J2
Plum Park La *TOW* NN12 .... 10 C3
Plumstead Av *BDWL* MK13.......... 2 C3
Plum Tree La *LBUZ* LU7 .... 84 B1
Plymouth Gv *EMV/FZ* MK4 .... 60 E2
Polmartin Ct *EAG/OLD/WT* MK6 ... 3 J7
Polruan Pl *EAG/OLD/WT* MK6 ..... 3 J7
Pomander Crs *WTR/OFPK* MK7 ... 51 G2
Pomfret Rd *TOW* NN12................ 5 F3
Pond Cl *RMKS/WB* MK17 .... 69 F3
Pondgate *WTR/OFPK* MK7 .... 51 G1
Poplar Cl *LBUZ* LU7 .... 80 B5
  TOW NN12 .... 5 F5
Poplars Rd *BUCK/WIN* MK18 ..... 55 G3
Porlock La *EMV/FZ* MK4 .... 49 F5
Portchester Ct
  CNH/GTH/TM MK8 .... 36 C6 🔢
Porter's Cl *RMKN* MK19 .... 33 K3
Portfield Cl *BUCK/WIN* MK18 ..... 55 G3
Portfields Rd *NPAG* MK16 .... 25 K1
Portfield Wy *BUCK/WIN* MK18 ... 55 H3
Porthcawl Gn *EMV/FZ* MK4 ...... 61 F3
Porthleven Pl *EAG/OLD/WT* MK6.. 3 J5
Porthmellin Cl *EMV/FZ* MK4 .... 60 E3 🔢
Portishead Dr *EMV/FZ* MK4 ...... 60 C2
Portland Dr *WLLN* MK15 .... 26 B6

Portmarnock Cl *BTCHLY* MK3 .... 61 G3 🔢
Portrush Cl *BTCHLY* MK3............ 61 G3
Portway *CNH/GTH/TM* MK8 ...... 48 A4
  GTLIN MK14 .... 37 J3
  SHEN MK5 .... 36 E6
  WLLN MK15 .... 38 C2
Potters La *STSTR* MK11 .... 35 J3
Pound Cl *RMKN* MK19 .... 33 F3
Poundfield Rd *TOW* NN12 .... 21 K3
Pound Hl *RMKS/WB* MK17 .... 71 H4
Pounds Cl *RBEDW* MK43 .... 29 J4
Powis La *EMV/FZ* MK4 .... 48 B6
Precedent Dr *BDWL* MK13 .... 36 E5
Prentice Gv *SHEN* MK5 .... 48 E6
Presley Wy *CNH/GTH/TM* MK8 ... 48 B2
Prestwick Cl *BTCHLY* MK3 ...... 61 G4 🔢
Primatt Crs *SHEN* MK5 .... 48 E3
Primrose Rd *BDWL* MK13 .... 36 D3
Prince Philip Av *RBEDW* MK43... 28 E3
Princes Cl *LBUZ* LU7 .... 84 A1
Princes Wy *WEAT* MK2 .... 62 B3
Priors Pk *EMV/FZ* MK4 .... 61 G1
Priory Cl *NPAG* MK16 .... 26 D1
Priory St *NPAG* MK16 .... 26 D1
Prospect Cl *RMKS/WB* MK17 ..... 77 F1
Prospect Pl *RMKN* MK19............ 13 G6
Prospect Rd *STSTR* MK11 .... 34 D2
Protheroe Fld *WTR/OFPK* MK7 ... 51 J5
Pulborough Cl *BTCHLY* MK3 ... 61 G2 🔢
Pulford Rd *LBUZ* LU7 .... 84 A3
Pumpus Gn *BUCK/WIN* MK18 ... 74 B3 🔢
Purbeck *GTLIN* MK14 .... 25 F6
Purcel Dr *NPAG* MK16 .... 26 A2
Pury Rd *TOW* NN12 .... 7 G6
Puxley Rd *RMKN* MK19 .... 33 J2
Pyke Hayes *CNH/GTH/TM* MK8 ... 36 A4
Pyxe Ct *WTR/OFPK* MK7 .... 51 F5

Q

Quadrans Cl *WLLN* MK15 .... 25 K6 🔢
Quantock Crs *EMV/FZ* MK4 .... 61 G1
Queen Anne St *BDWL* MK13....... 24 C6
Queen Eleanor St *STSTR* MK11 ... 34 E1
Queens Av *NPAG* MK16 .... 26 B1
Queen's Rd *TOW* NN12 .... 5 F3
Queen St *LBUZ* LU7 .... 84 A1
  STSTR MK11 .... 35 F1
Queensway *WEAT* MK2 .... 62 B3
Quilter Meadow
  WTR/OFPK MK7 .... 51 J4 🔢
Quinton Dr *BDWL* MK13 .... 36 D4

R

Rackstraw Gv *WTR/OFPK* MK7 ... 51 J4
Radcliffe St *WOLV* MK12 .... 24 A6 🔢
Radclive Rd *BUCK/WIN* MK18..... 54 C5
Radman Gv *WOLV* MK12 .... 35 K2
Radworthy *EMV/FZ* MK4 .... 49 F6
Rainbow Dr *EAG/OLD/WT* MK6 ... 49 J2
Rainsborough *GTLIN* MK14 ...... 25 K5 🔢
Ramsay Cl *BDWL* MK13 .... 36 E4
Ramsgill Ct *BDWL* MK13 .... 37 F3
Ramsons Av *GTLIN* MK14 .... 3 F1
Ramsthorn Gv *WTR/OFPK* MK7 .. 51 G3 🔢
Ranelagh Gdns *NPAG* MK16 .... 26 B3 🔢
Rangers Ct *CNH/GTH/TM* MK8.... 36 C6
Rannock Cl *WEAT* MK2 .... 62 C6
Rannock Gdns *LBUZ* LU7 .... 83 H2 🔢
Rashleigh Pl *EAG/OLD/WT* MK6 ... 49 H2
Rathbone Cl *CNH/GTH/TM* MK8 ... 48 B2
Ravel Cl *WTR/OFPK* MK7 .... 51 J3
Ravensbourne Pl
  EAG/OLD/WT MK6................. 38 A5
Ravenscar Ct *EMV/FZ* MK4........ 61 F2
Ravigill Pl *WOLV* MK12.............. 36 A3
Rawlins Rd *BDWL* MK13 .... 36 D5
Rayleigh Cl *SHEN* MK5 .... 48 E3 🔢
Reach Gn *LBUZ* LU7 .... 80 B1
Reach La *LBUZ* LU7 .... 80 D2
Rectory Flds *WLLN* MK15 .... 38 C4 🔢
Redbridge *GTLIN* MK14 .... 25 G6
Redcote Mnr *WTR/OFPK* MK7 ... 51 F5
Redding Gv *CNH/GTH/TM* MK8 ... 48 A2
Red House Cl *RMKS/WB* MK17 ... 69 G1 🔢
Redhuish Cl *EMV/FZ* MK4 .... 49 G6
Redland Dr *SHEN* MK5 .... 48 E2
Red Lion Cl *RBEDW* MK43 .... 29 J4 🔢
Redmoor *TOW* NN12 .... 4 E5 🔢
Redshaw Cl *BUCK/WIN* MK18 ... 55 H2
Redvers Ga *WLLN* MK15 .... 26 A6
Redwood Ga *SHEN* MK5 .... 49 F5
Redwood Gld *LBUZ* LU7 .... 80 A4

Regent St *LBUZ* LU7 ....
  WEAT MK2 ....
Reliance La *CMK* MK9 ....
Rendlesham *WLLN* MK15 ....
Reynolds Cl *RBEDW* MK43 ....
Rhodes Pl *EAG/OLD/WT* MK6 ....
Rhondda Cl *DBGH* MK1 ....
Rhoscolyn Dr *EMV/FZ* MK4 ......
Rhuddlan Cl *SHEN* MK5.............
Ribble Cl *NPAG* MK16 ....
Ribble Crs *BTCHLY* MK3 ....
Richardson Pl *EAG/OLD/WT* MK6
Richborough *BDWL* MK13 ....
Richmond Cl *BTCHLY* MK3 ....
Richmond Rd *LBUZ* LU7 ....
  TOW NN12 ....
Richmond Wy *NPAG* MK16 ....
Rickley La *BTCHLY* MK3 ....
Rickyard Cl *BDWL* MK13 ....
Ridgeway *LBUZ* LU7 ....
  RMKN MK19 ....
  STSTR MK11 ....
  WOLV MK12 ....
Ridgmont *RMKN* MK19 ....
Ridgmont Rd *RBEDW* MK43........
Ridgway *RMKS/WB* MK17 ....
The Riding *RMKN* MK19 ....
Rillington Gdns *EMV/FZ* MK4 .....
Rimsdale Ct *WEAT* MK2 ....
Rivercrest Rd *RMKN* MK19 ....
Riverside *LBUZ* LU7 ....
River Side *NPAG* MK16...............
Rixband Cl *WTR/OFPK* MK7 ....
Roberson Cl *TOW* NN12 ....
Robertson Cl *SHEN* MK5 ....
Robeson Pl *CNH/GTH/TM* MK8 ...
Robin Cl *BUCK/WIN* MK18 ....
  TOW NN12 ....
Robins Hl *EAG/OLD/WT* MK6 .....
Robinswood Cl *LBUZ* LU7 ....
Roche Gdns *BTCHLY* MK3 ....
Rochester Ct *SHEN* MK5 ....
Rochfords *EAG/OLD/WT* MK6 .....
Rock Cl *LBUZ* LU7 ....
Rockingham Dr *GTLIN* MK14 ......
Rock La *LBUZ* LU7 ....
Rockspray Gv *WTR/OFPK* MK7 ...
Rodwell Gdns *WTR/OFPK* MK7 ...
Roebuck Wy *SHEN* MK5 ....
Roeburn Crs *EMV/FZ* MK4 ....
Rogers Cft *EMV/FZ* MK4 ....
Rolvenden Gv *WTR/OFPK* MK7 ...
Romar Ct *DBGH* MK1 ....
Rooksley *BDWL* MK13 ....
Roosevelt Av *LBUZ* LU7 ....
Rosebay Cl *WTR/OFPK* MK7 ......
Rosebery Av *LBUZ* LU7 ....
Rosecomb Pl *SHEN* MK5 ....
Rosemary Ct *WTR/OFPK* MK7 ....
Rosemullion Av *EMV/FZ* MK4 ....
Roslyn Ct *WLLN* MK15 ....
Rossal Pl *WOLV* MK12 ....
Rossendale *GTLIN* MK14 ....
Rossini Pl *WTR/OFPK* MK7 ....
Ross Wy *BTCHLY* MK3 ....
Rothersthorpe *GTLIN* MK14 ....
Rothschild Rd *LBUZ* LU7 ....
Rotten Rw *RMKS/WB* MK17 ....
Rovers Cft *WOLV* MK12 ....
Rowan Cl *TOW* NN12 ....
Rowan Dr *RMKN* MK19 ....
Rowan Wy *RBEDW* MK43 ....
Rowlands Cl *WEAT* MK2 ....
Rowle Cl *GTLIN* MK14 ....
Rowley Furrows *LBUZ* LU7 ....
Rowsham Dell *GTLIN* MK14 ....
Roxburgh Wy *BTCHLY* MK3 ....
Royce Rd *RBEDW* MK43 ....
Rubbra Cl *WTR/OFPK* MK7 ....
Rudchesters *BDWL* MK13 ....
Rudds Cl *BUCK/WIN* MK18 ....
The Ruins *TOW* NN12 ....
Rumbold's St *BUCK/WIN* MK18 ..
Runford Ct *SHEN* MK5.................
Runnymede *GTLIN* MK14 ....
Rushleys Cl *SHEN* MK5 ....
Rushmere Cl *RMKS/WB* MK17 .....
Rushton Ct *CNH/GTH/TM* MK8 ...
Ruskin Cl *NPAG* MK16 ....
Rusland Circ *EMV/FZ* MK4 ....
Russell St *RMKS/WB* MK17 ....
Russell Wy *LBUZ* LU7 ....
Rutherford Ga *SHEN* MK5 ....
Ruthven Cl *WEAT* MK2 ....
Rycroft *EMV/FZ* MK4 ....
Rydal Wy *WEAT* MK2 ....
Rye Cl *LBUZ* LU7 ....
Ryeland *STSTR* MK11 ....

...e Cl *BDWL* MK13 ...... 36 E4
...*EMV/FZ* MK4 ...... 49 F6

S

...Pl *GTLIN* MK14 ...... 37 K2
...Gn *RMKS/WB* MK17 ...... 52 C4
...St *WEAT* MK2 ...... 62 C4
...'s Rd *BUCK/WIN* MK18 .. 74 A3
...ws Cl *LBUZ* LU7 ...... 84 B2
...w Rd *BTCHLY* MK3 ...... 61 H4
...w's St *LBUZ* LU7 ...... 84 B2
...nys Pl *EMV/FZ* MK4 ...... 60 E4
...*WTR/OFPK* MK7 ...... 39 C6
...ohs *WTR/OFPK* MK7 ...... 39 C6
...Cl *EAG/OLD/WT* MK6.... 38 B5
...rine's Av *BTCHLY* MK3 ...... 61 G5
...nt's Dr *BTCHLY* MK3 ...... 61 G5
...s Rd *BTCHLY* MK3 ...... 61 H5
...rds Ct *GTLIN* MK14 ...... 25 J6
...ns Cl *RMKS/WB* MK17 ...... 69 G2
...e's Cl *LBUZ* LU7 ...... 84 C1
...N12 ...... 5 F4
...e's Rd *BTCHLY* MK3 ...... 61 G5
...s Wy *WOLV* MK12 ...... 24 A6
...Ms *STSTR* MK11 ...... 34 C1
...*BDWL* MK13 ...... 24 C6
...s Cl *EMV/FZ* MK4 ...... 61 F3
...Cl *RMKN* MK19 ...... 13 H1
...st *BDWL* MK13 ...... 24 C6
...Cl *LBUZ* LU7 ...... 85 K4
...Crs *WOLV* MK12 ...... 36 A2
...La *RMKN* MK19 ...... 33 G3
...s Rd *BTCHLY* MK3 ...... 61 G5
...N12 ...... 5 F5
...nce Rd Sout
...N12 ...... 5 F5
...nce Vw *BDWL* MK13 ... 36 D3
...Dr *GTLIN* MK14 ...... 25 H6
...rd's Cl *LBUZ* LU7 ...... 80 C4
...ret Ct *WEAT* MK2 ...... 62 D3
...rets Cl *RMKS/WB* MK16.. 26 D1
...'s St *WEAT* MK2 ...... 62 B3
...s Av *BTCHLY* MK3 ...... 61 H4
...MK11 ...... 34 E1
...s Cl *RMKS/WB* MK17 ...... 51 K2
...WB MK17 ...... 76 A1
...s Wy *LBUZ* LU7 ...... 83 K2
...ews Cl *BTCHLY* MK3 ... 61 H5
...els Cl *LBUZ* LU7 ...... 77 H6
...'s Wy *BTCHLY* MK3 ...... 61 H5
...Rd *BTCHLY* MK3 ...... 61 H5
...y *BDWL* MK13 ...... 24 D5
...as Ct *EMV/FZ* MK4 ...... 60 C2
...ns *RMKS/WB* MK17 ...... 52 D5
...*RMKS/WB* MK17 ...... 77 F1
...MK5 ...... 48 E3
...rd *RMKS/WB* MK17 ...... 41 H6
...Gv *GTLIN* MK14 ...... 25 J3
...s *GTLIN* MK14 ...... 37 J1
...k *EMV/FZ* MK4 ...... 60 E1
...e Ct *WTR/OFPK* MK7 ... 51 F3
...t *SHEN* MK5 ...... 48 D4
...*WTR/OFPK* MK7 ...... 51 F3
...La *TOW* NN12 ...... 21 J2
...*LBUZ* LU7 ...... 80 B6
...st Dr *BUCK/WIN* MK18 ... 55 F4
...Ct *BTCHLY* MK3 ...... 61 G5
...ham Cl *TOW* NN12 ...... 4 E5
...ham Pl *WEAT* MK2 ...... 62 B3
...Ct *CNH/GTH/TM* MK8 ... 35 K5
...s *GTLIN* MK14 ...... 25 C5
...me Rd *TOW* NN12 ...... 4 E4
...*LBUZ* LU7 ...... 80 B4
...WB MK17 ...... 64 C1
...ell Dr *WLLN* MK15 ...... 37 K1
...o Rd *RMKS/WB* MK17 ...... 53 C5
...v *WEAT* MK2 ...... 70 C1
...*LBUZ* LU7 ...... 84 E1
...s Cl *WTR/OFPK* MK7 ... 51 J3
...a *CMK* MK9 ...... 3 F5
...l *LBUZ* LU7 ...... 84 D2
...*BDWL* MK13 ...... 25 F6
...D/WT MK6 ...... 49 K2
...MK2 ...... 62 B2
...*BDWL* MK13 ...... 36 E2
...Cl *BDWL* MK13 ...... 36 D3
...*TOW* NN12 ...... 4 A1
...r *RMKS/WB* MK17 ...... 69 F2
...nd *RMKS/WB* MK17 ...... 66 B2
...a *BUCK/WIN* MK18 ...... 55 F3
...MK16 ...... 17 F1

RBEDW MK43 ...... 53 J4
RMKN MK19 ...... 13 G6
RMKS/WB MK17 ...... 70 C5
SHEN MK5 ...... 48 E1
TOW NN12 ...... 4 A1
TOW NN12 ...... 11 K5
School St *BDWL* MK13 ...... 24 C6
Schumann Ct *WTR/OFPK* MK7 ... 51 H5
Scotney Gdns *BTCHLY* MK3 ...... 61 H3
Scott Dr *NPAG* MK16 ...... 15 G4
Scotts Cl *RMKS/WB* MK17 ...... 70 D5
Scotts Farm Cl *BUCK/WIN* MK18 .. 43 H5
Scotts La *BUCK/WIN* MK18 ...... 43 H6
Scriveners La *TOW* NN12 ...... 9 J3
Seagrave Ct *WTR/OFPK* MK7 ...... 50 E5
Secklow Ga *CMK* MK9 ...... 3 G4
Second Av *DBGH* MK1 ...... 62 B1
Sedgemere *CNH/GTH/TM* MK8 .. 36 A5
Selbourne Av *BTCHLY* MK3 ...... 61 J4
Selby Gv *SHEN* MK5 ...... 48 D4
Selkirk Gv *BTCHLY* MK3 ...... 61 J1
Selworthy *EMV/FZ* MK4 ...... 49 G6
Serjeants Gn *GTLIN* MK14 ...... 37 J1
Serles Cl *EAG/OLD/WT* MK6 ...... 49 K3
Severn Dr *NPAG* MK16 ...... 26 C1
Severn Wy *BTCHLY* MK3 ...... 61 G3
Shackleton Pl *EAG/OLD/WT* MK6 ... 3 F7
Shaftesbury Ct
   BUCK/WIN MK18 ...... 74 A2
Shaftesbury Crs *BTCHLY* MK3 ...... 61 K2
Shakespeare Cl *NPAG* MK16 ...... 15 K6
Shamrock Cl *WTR/OFPK* MK7 ... 51 G3
Shannon Ct *GTLIN* MK14 ...... 37 K1
Sharkham Ct *EMV/FZ* MK4 ...... 60 E2
Sharman Wk *BDWL* MK13 ...... 36 D4
Shaw Cl *NPAG* MK16 ...... 15 J6
Shearmans *STSTR* MK11 ...... 35 H3
Sheelin Gv *WEAT* MK2 ...... 70 C1
Sheepcoat Cl *SHEN* MK5 ...... 48 D4
Sheepcote Cl *LBUZ* LU7 ...... 80 B2
Sheep St *BUCK/WIN* MK18 ...... 74 B3
Sheldon Ct *CNH/GTH/TM* MK8 .. 36 C6
   RMKS/WB MK17 ...... 52 C5
Shelley Cl *NPAG* MK16 ...... 26 A1
   TOW NN12 ...... 4 E4
Shelley Dr *BTCHLY* MK3 ...... 61 J4
Shelsmore *GTLIN* MK14 ...... 25 K5
Shenley Cl *LBUZ* LU7 ...... 80 C4
Shenley Hill Rd *LBUZ* LU7 ...... 80 C4
Shenley Rd *BTCHLY* MK3 ...... 61 H2
   RMKS/WB MK17 ...... 59 K3
   SHEN MK5 ...... 48 D2
Shepherds *STSTR* MK11 ...... 35 H3
Shepherds Md *LBUZ* LU7 ...... 80 B6
Shepherds Rw
   BUCK/WIN MK18 ...... 74 B3
Sheppards Cl *NPAG* MK16 ...... 26 B1
Shepperds Gn *SHEN* MK5 ...... 48 C5
Shepperton Ct *RMKN* MK19 ...... 13 F6
Sherbourne Dr *WTR/OFPK* MK7 ... 51 G6
Sherington Rd *NPAG* MK16 ...... 16 E3
Shernfold *WTR/OFPK* MK7 ...... 51 G2
Sherwood Dr *BTCHLY* MK3 ...... 62 A2
Shilling Cl *WLLN* MK15 ...... 25 K6
Shipley Rd *NPAG* MK16 ...... 25 K1
Shipman Ct *WLLN* MK15 ...... 26 A6
Ship Rd *LBUZ* LU7 ...... 83 K3
Shipton Hl *BDWL* MK13 ...... 36 E1
Shire La *NPAG* MK16 ...... 28 E1
Shirley Moor *WTR/OFPK* MK7 ...... 51 G1
Shirrell Crs *EMV/FZ* MK4 ...... 49 G4
Shorham Ri *CNH/GTH/TM* MK8 ... 36 B5
Shouler Cl *SHEN* MK5 ...... 48 D4
Showsley Rd *TOW* NN12 ...... 6 C1
Shucklow Hl *RMKS/WB* MK17 ...... 66 E2
Shutlanger Rd *TOW* NN12 ...... 7 F1
Shuttleworth Gv *WTR/OFPK* MK7.. 51 J3
Sidlaw Ct *STSTR* MK11 ...... 35 G3
Silbury Bvd *CMK* MK9 ...... 2 C5
Silicon Ct *SHEN* MK5 ...... 49 F4
Silverbirches La *RMKS/WB* MK17 .. 64 B1
Silver St *NPAG* MK16 ...... 26 C1
   STSTR MK11 ...... 34 E2
Silverweed Ct *WTR/OFPK* MK7 .. 51 G4
Simdims *RBEDW* MK43 ...... 29 H4
Simnel Cl *LBUZ* LU7 ...... 80 A4
Simonsbath *EMV/FZ* MK4 ...... 61 G1
Simons Lea *BDWL* MK13 ...... 36 E3
Simpson Dr *EAG/OLD/WT* MK6 ... 50 D4
Simpson Rd *EAG/OLD/WT* MK6 ... 50 D4
Sinclair Dr *DBGH* MK1 ...... 50 A6
Singleborough La
   RMKS/WB MK17 ...... 66 A2
Sipthorp Cl *WTR/OFPK* MK7 ... 51 H3
Sitwell Cl *NPAG* MK16 ...... 15 J6
Skeats Whf *WLLN* MK15 ...... 25 K6
Skeldon Ga *GTLIN* MK14 ...... 37 K3
Skene Cl *WEAT* MK2 ...... 70 B1

Skipton Cl *WLLN* MK15 ...... 38 B1
Slade La *STSTR* MK11 ...... 35 H3
The Slade *RMKS/WB* MK17 ...... 69 G2
   TOW NN12 ...... 8 B6
Slated Rw *WOLV* MK12 ...... 23 H6
Smabridge Wk *WLLN* MK15 ...... 26 C6
Small Crs *BUCK/WIN* MK18 ...... 55 J5
Smarden Bell *WTR/OFPK* MK7 ... 51 G1
Smeaton Cl *GTLIN* MK14 ...... 25 K3
Smithergill Ct *GTLIN* MK14 ...... 37 F2
Smithfield End *RMKS/WB* MK17 ... 75 G3
Smithland Ct *TOW* NN12 ...... 4 A1
Smithsons Pl *CMK* MK9 ...... 3 K6
Snaith Crs *SHEN* MK5 ...... 48 E2
Snelshall St *EMV/FZ* MK4 ...... 60 C3
Snowberry Cl *WOLV* MK12 ...... 36 A2
Snowdon Dr *EAG/OLD/WT* MK6... 49 C2
Snowshill Ct *GTLIN* MK14 ...... 25 J3
Sokeman Cl *WOLV* MK12 ...... 35 H2
Solar Ct *GTLIN* MK14 ...... 25 H4
Solly's Wy *TOW* NN12 ...... 5 F4
Somerset Cl *BTCHLY* MK3 ...... 61 J2
Sorrell Dr *NPAG* MK16 ...... 25 J1
Soskin Dr *GTLIN* MK14 ...... 37 G1
Soulbury Rd *LBUZ* LU7 ...... 77 J6
Southbridge Gv *WTR/OFPK* MK7... 51 F2
Southcott Village *LBUZ* LU7 ... 83 J3
Southcourt Av *LBUZ* LU7 ...... 83 J3
Southcourt Rd *LBUZ* LU7 ...... 83 J2
South Eighth St *CMK* MK9 ...... 3 F5
Southern Wy *WOLV* MK12 ...... 35 H1
Southfield Cl *WLLN* MK15 ...... 26 D6
South Fifth St *CMK* MK9 ...... 2 E6
South Fourth St *CMK* MK9 ...... 2 D7
Southgate Dr *TOW* NN12 ...... 5 G4
South Grafton *EAG/OLD/WT* MK6.. 49 C1
South Lawne *BTCHLY* MK3 ...... 61 J3
South Ninth St *CMK* MK9 ...... 3 G5
South Rw *CMK* MK9 ...... 2 E7
South Saxon *EAG/OLD/WT* MK6 .. 3 G6
South Secklow *CMK* MK9 ...... 3 H5
South Second St *CMK* MK9 ...... 2 C7
South Seventh St *CMK* MK9 ...... 2 E6
South Sixth St *CMK* MK9 ...... 2 E6
South St *LBUZ* LU7 ...... 84 C2
   RMKN MK19 ...... 13 H6
South Tenth St *CMK* MK9 ...... 3 G5
South Ter *WEAT* MK2 ...... 62 B3
Southwick Ct
   CNH/GTH/TM MK8 ...... 48 C1
South Witan *CMK* MK9 ...... 2 E7
Sovereign Dr *WLLN* MK15 ...... 25 K6
Spark Wy *NPAG* MK16 ...... 15 J6
Sparsholt Ct *EMV/FZ* MK4 ...... 61 F1
Spearmint Ct *WTR/OFPK* MK7 .. 51 H4
Specklands *SHEN* MK5 ...... 48 D2
Speedwell Pl *GTLIN* MK14 ...... 37 H3
Speldhurst Ct *WTR/OFPK* MK7 .. 51 G2
Spencer *GTLIN* MK14 ...... 25 F5
Spenlows Rd *BTCHLY* MK3 ...... 49 K6
Spinney Cl *TOW* NN12 ...... 5 F6
Spinney La *RMKS/WB* MK17 ...... 53 F5
The Spinney *BDWL* MK13 ...... 36 D3
   BUCK/WIN MK18 ...... 74 B1
Sponnes Rd *TOW* NN12 ...... 5 F4
Spoonley Wd *BDWL* MK13 ...... 36 B2
Spring Cl *RMKS/WB* MK17 ...... 66 A3
Springfield *EAG/OLD/WT* MK6 ...... 3 K4
Springfield Bvd
   EAG/OLD/WT MK6 ...... 38 A5
Springfield Gdns *RMKN* MK19 ...... 33 K3
Springfield Rd *LBUZ* LU7 ...... 83 J2
Springfields *TOW* NN12 ...... 4 E4
Springfield Wy *RBEDW* MK43 ...... 29 K3
Spring Gdns *NPAG* MK16 ...... 26 B1
Spring Gv *RMKS/WB* MK17 ...... 52 C4
Spring La *RMKS/WB* MK17 ...... 66 B3
   TOW NN12 ...... 6 E6
The Square *WOLV* MK12 ...... 36 A1
Squires Cl *EAG/OLD/WT* MK6 ...... 49 K3
Squirrels Wy *BUCK/WIN* MK18 ...... 55 H4
Stacey Av *WOLV* MK12 ...... 36 A1
Stafford Gv *SHEN* MK5 ...... 48 E3
Stainton Dr *BDWL* MK13 ...... 37 F3
Stamford Av *EAG/OLD/WT* MK6 ... 38 A5
Stanbridge Rd *LBUZ* LU7 ...... 84 C3
Stanbridge Road Ter *LBUZ* LU7 ... 84 C3
Stanbrook Rd *WTR/OFPK* MK7 ... 39 F6
Standing Wy *BTCHLY* MK3 ...... 60 E4
   EAG/OLD/WT MK6 ...... 50 C2
   MKV MK10 ...... 39 H6
   RMKS/WB MK17 ...... 39 H6
   RMKS/WB MK17 ...... 60 C5
Stanmore Gdns *NPAG* MK16 ...... 26 A3
Stanton Av *BDWL* MK13 ...... 36 D1
Stanton Ga *GTLIN* MK14 ...... 25 C5
Stanton Wd *BDWL* MK13 ...... 37 G3
Stanway Cl *WLLN* MK15 ...... 38 A1

Staple Hall Rd *DBGH* MK1 ...... 62 C2
Staters Pound *WLLN* MK15 ...... 25 K6
Statham Pl *EAG/OLD/WT* MK6 ...... 49 J1
Station Rd *BUCK/WIN* MK18 ...... 55 F4
   BUCK/WIN MK18 ...... 74 A2
   LBUZ LU7 ...... 83 K2
   NPAG MK16 ...... 26 B1
   RMKN MK19 ...... 13 F6
   RMKS/WB MK17 ...... 52 C5
   RMKS/WB MK17 ...... 63 G1
   RMKS/WB MK17 ...... 67 H6
   RMKS/WB MK17 ...... 75 G2
   RMKS/WB MK17 ...... 75 H4
Stavordale *WTR/OFPK* MK7 ...... 39 F6
Steinbeck Crs *EMV/FZ* MK4 ...... 60 C2
Stephenson Cl *LBUZ* LU7 ...... 83 K3
Steppingstone Pl *LBUZ* LU7 ...... 84 C3
Stevens Fld *WTR/OFPK* MK7 ...... 51 J3
Stewart Dr *TOW* NN12 ...... 18 A1
Stewkley La *RMKS/WB* MK17 ...... 76 B3
Stewkley Rd *LBUZ* LU7 ...... 78 B5
The Stile *LBUZ* LU7 ...... 80 B2
Stirling Cl *WLLN* MK15 ...... 37 K1
Stockdale *BDWL* MK13 ...... 37 F2
Stockhall Crs *LBUZ* LU7 ...... 77 G5
Stock La *RMKS/WB* MK17 ...... 59 J2
Stocks Hl *TOW* NN12 ...... 8 A6
The Stocks *RMKN* MK19 ...... 23 F3
Stockwell La *RMKS/WB* MK17 ...... 51 J1
Stoke La *RMKS/WB* MK17 ...... 71 H4
Stokenchurch Pl *BDWL* MK13 ...... 2 B1
Stoke Rd *LBUZ* LU7 ...... 79 K6
   RMKS/WB MK17 ...... 69 H2
   RNHPTN NN7 ...... 7 K1
   WEAT MK2 ...... 62 D6
Stonecrop Pl *GTLIN* MK14... ...... 2 E1
Stonegate *BDWL* MK13 ...... 36 D2
Stone Hl *CNH/GTH/TM* MK8 ...... 36 A6
Stones Wy *RMKS/WB* MK17 ...... 77 F1
Stonor Ct *CNH/GTH/TM* MK8 ... 48 C1
Stony Hl *TOW* NN12 ...... 10 A3
Stotfold Ct *STSTR* MK11 ...... 35 F3
Stour Cl *BTCHLY* MK3 ...... 61 H3
   NPAG MK16 ...... 26 D2
Stowe Av *BUCK/WIN* MK18 ...... 42 D4
Stowe Cl *BUCK/WIN* MK18 ...... 55 F2
Stowe Ri *BUCK/WIN* MK18 ...... 55 F2
Strangford Dr *WEAT* MK2 ...... 70 B1
Stratfield Ct
   CNH/GTH/TM MK8 ...... 36 C6
Stratford Rd *BUCK/WIN* MK18 ...... 55 K1
   RMKN MK19 ...... 22 E4
   RMKS/WB MK17 ...... 47 H6
   WOLV MK12 ...... 23 K6
Strathnaver Pl *WOLV* MK12 ...... 36 A3
Stratton Ms *LBUZ* LU7 ...... 84 C2
Strauss Gv *WTR/OFPK* MK7 ...... 51 H5
Streatham Pl *BDWL* MK13 ...... 2 A4
Stringfellow Cl *RBEDW* MK43 ...... 29 F3
Strudwick Dr *EAG/OLD/WT* MK6 ... 49 J1
Stuart Cl *WEAT* MK2 ...... 62 C2
Studley Knapp *WTR/OFPK* MK7... 51 G3
Sturges Cl *WTR/OFPK* MK7 ...... 51 F4
Sulgrave Ct
   CNH/GTH/TM MK8 ...... 48 C1
Sullivan Crs *WTR/OFPK* MK7 ...... 51 H5
Sultan Cft *SHEN* MK5 ...... 48 D5
Summergill Ct *BDWL* MK13 ...... 37 F2
Summerhayes *GTLIN* MK14 ...... 25 J6
Summerson Rd
   EAG/OLD/WT MK6 ...... 49 J4
Summer St *LBUZ* LU7 ...... 84 C2
Sumner Ct *SHEN* MK5 ...... 48 D1
Sunbury Cl *BDWL* MK13 ...... 36 D1
Sunderland Ct *EMV/FZ* MK4 ...... 60 C2
Sunningdale Wy *BTCHLY* MK3 ...... 61 F3
Sunridge Cl *NPAG* MK16 ...... 26 B2
Sunrise Pkwy *GTLIN* MK14 ...... 37 H1
Sunset Cl *WEAT* MK2 ...... 62 B4
Sun Yd *TOW* NN12 ...... 5 G4
Surrey Pl *BTCHLY* MK3 ...... 61 J1
Surrey Rd *BTCHLY* MK3 ...... 61 J1
Surtees Wy *TOW* NN12 ...... 5 F2
Sussex Rd *BTCHLY* MK3 ...... 61 J2
Sutcliffe Av *EAG/OLD/WT* MK6 ...... 2 E7
Sutherland Gv *BTCHLY* MK3 ...... 49 J6
Sutleye Ct *SHEN* MK5 ...... 48 D4
Sutton Ct *EMV/FZ* MK4 ...... 61 F2
Swallow Cl *BUCK/WIN* MK18 ...... 55 H4
Swallowfield *CNH/GTH/TM* MK8.. 36 B6
Swanbourne Rd *RMKS/WB* MK17.. 75 K3
Swan Cl *BUCK/WIN* MK18 ...... 55 H4
Sweetlands Cnr *WTR/OFPK* MK7.. 51 G1
Swift Cl *NPAG* MK16 ...... 15 K6
Swimbridge La *EMV/FZ* MK4 ...... 49 G5
Swinneyford Rd *TOW* NN12 ...... 5 F4
Sycamore Av *WEAT* MK2 ...... 62 D5
Sycamore Cl *BUCK/WIN* MK18 ...... 55 J4

LBUZ LU7 .... **77** G5
TOW NN12 .... **5** F5
Sycamore Rd *TOW* NN12 .... **4** B1
Sykes Cft *EMV/FZ* MK4 .... **61** F2
Sylvester St *LBUZ* LU7 .... **84** B1
Symington Ct *SHEN* MK5 .... **48** E4 🔲
Syon Gdns *NPAG* MK16 .... **26** B3
Syowe Ct *GTLIN* MK14 .... **25** F5

T

Tabard Gdns *NPAC* MK16 .... **26** B3 🔲
Tacknell Dr *SHEN* MK5................... **48** C5
Tadmarton *GTLIN* MK14 .... **37** K1
Tadmere *CNH/GTH/TM* MK8 .... **36** A6 🔲
Talbot Ct *LBUZ* LU7 .... **84** B1
WLLN MK15 .... **38** B6
Talland Av *EAG/OLD/WT* MK6..... **3** H6
Tallis La *WTR/OFPK* MK7 .... **51** H4
Tamarisk Ct *WTR/OFPK* MK7 .... **51** G4
Tattam Ct *WLLN* MK15 .... **38** B5
Tamworth Stubb
WTR/OFPK MK7 .... **51** F4
Tandra *EAG/OLD/WT* MK6............ **50** A4
Tanfield La *MKV* MK10.................. **39** F4
Tank House Rd *BUCK/WIN* MK18.... **74** C2
Tanners Dr *GTLIN* MK14............... **25** K3
Tansman La *WTR/OFPK* MK7 .... **51** J4 🔲
Taranis Cl *WTR/OFPK* MK7............ **51** H2
Tarnbrook La *EMV/FZ* MK4 .... **60** E1 🔲
Tarragon Cl *WTR/OFPK* MK7 .... **51** F3 🔲
Tatling Gv *WTR/OFPK* MK7 .... **51** F4
Tattam Ct *WLLN* MK15 .... **38** B5
Tattams La *RMKS/WB* MK17 .... **75** J4
Tattenhoe La *BTCHLY* MK3 .... **61** H4
Tattenhoe St *CNH/GTH/TM* MK8 .. **48** A4
EMV/FZ MK4 .... **48** C6
Tattershall Cl *SHEN* MK5 .... **48** D3
Taunton Deane *EMV/FZ* MK4 .... **61** G1
Tavelhurst *CNH/GTH/TM* MK8 ..... **36** B6
Taverner Cl *WTR/OFPK* MK7 .... **51** J4 🔲
Tavistock Cl *RMKS/WB* MK17 .... **52** B3
Tavistock St *WEAT* MK2 .... **62** B2
Taylors Ms *GTLIN* MK14 .... **37** J1
Taylor's Ride *LBUZ* LU7 .... **80** A5
Taymouth Pl *CMK* MK9 .... **38** A4
Tay Rd *BTCHLY* MK3 .... **61** H2
Teasel Av *GTLIN* MK14 .... **37** H2
Tees Wy *BTCHLY* MK3 .... **61** G2
Teign Cl *NPAG* MK16..................... **26** C1
Telford Wy *GTLIN* MK14................ **26** A4
Temple *GTLIN* MK14 .... **25** F6
Temple Cl *BTCHLY* MK3 .... **61** G4
BUCK/WIN MK18 .... **55** H1
Tene Acres *SHEN* MK5 .... **48** C3
Tennis La *BUCK/WIN* MK18 .... **74** B4
Tennyson Cl *TOW* NN12 .... **4** E4
Tennyson Dr *NPAG* MK16 .... **25** K1
Tennyson Gv *BTCHLY* MK3 .... **61** J4
Tenterden Crs *WTR/OFPK* MK7 .. **51** G2 🔲
Tewkesbury La *MKV* MK10 .... **38** E6
Tews End La *TOW* NN12 .... **10** A3
Thames Cl *BTCHLY* MK3 .... **61** H3
Thames Dr *NPAG* MK16 .... **26** C2
Thane Ct *GTLIN* MK14................... **25** F6
Theydon Av *RMKS/WB* MK17 .... **52** C5
Third Av *DBGH* MK1 .... **62** A1
Thirlby La *SHEN* MK5..................... **48** D3
Thirlmere Av *WEAT* MK2 .... **62** C5
Thirsk Gdns *RMKS/WB* MK17 .... **61** F5
Thomas Dr *NPAG* MK16 .... **15** K6 🔲
Thomas St *LBUZ* LU7 .... **80** B2
Thompson St *BDWL* MK13 .... **24** D5 🔲
Thornborough Rd
RMKS/WB MK17 .... **58** A3
Thorncliffe *CNH/GTH/TM* MK8...... **36** A6
Thorneycroft La *WLLN* MK15........ **38** A2
Thornhill *BUCK/WIN* MK18 .... **57** G5
Thornley Cft *EMV/FZ* MK4 .... **61** F1
Thornton Rd *RMKN* MK19 .... **46** A3
RMKS/WB MK17 .... **58** B2
Thorwold Pl *SHEN* MK5 .... **48** E3 🔲
Three Shires Wy *NPAG* MK16 .... **15** F3
RMKN MK19 .... **14** C2
Thresher Gv *WOLV* MK12 .... **35** H2
Thrift Rd *LBUZ* LU7 .... **80** B2
Thrupp Cl *RMKN* MK19 .... **13** H5
Thurne Cl *NPAG* MK16 .... **26** D2 🔲
Thursby Rd *WLLN* MK15 .... **38** A2
Thyme Cl *NPAG* MK16 .... **15** J6
Ticehurst Cl *WTR/OFPK* MK7 .... **51** G2
Tickford St *NPAG* MK16 .... **26** C1
Tidbury Cl *RMKS/WB* MK17 .... **52** B5
Tiffany Cl *WEAT* MK2 .... **62** C5
Tilers Rd *STSTR* MK11 .... **35** J5
Tillman Cl *WOLV* MK12 .... **35** K2
Timber La *RMKS/WB* MK17 .... **65** F5

Timberscombe *EMV/FZ* MK4 ..... **49** G6 🔲
Timbold Dr *WTR/OFPK* MK7 .... **51** F1
Timbold Dr *WTR/OFPK* MK7 .... **50** E2
Tindall Av *LBUZ* LU7...................... **80** C6
Tingewick Rd *BUCK/WIN* MK18 .... **54** E3
Tinkers Dr *BUCK/WIN* MK18 .... **74** A4
Tintagel Ct *EAG/OLD/WT* MK6 ..... **49** K1
Tippet Cl *WTR/OFPK* MK7 .... **51** J5
Titchmarsh Ct *EAG/OLD/WT* MK6 .. **49** H1
Tolcarne Av *EAG/OLD/WT* MK6 ..... **3** K6
Tompkins Cl *SHEN* MK5 .... **48** C5
Tongwell La *NPAG* MK16 .... **26** B4
Tongwell St *MKV* MK10 .... **38** E3
WLLN MK15 .... **26** D5
WTR/OFPK MK7 .... **51** H4
Top Angel *BUCK/WIN* MK18 .... **55** G6
Top Meadow *WTR/OFPK* MK7 ...... **51** G6
Torre Cl *BTCHLY* MK3 .... **61** K1
Torridon Ct *WEAT* MK2 .... **70** C1
Tove La *TOW* NN12 .... **4** D3
Towan Av *EAG/OLD/WT* MK6 .... **3** J7
Towcester Dr *TOW* NN12 .... **21** G2
Towcester Rd *BUCK/WIN* MK18..... **43** H5
RMKN MK19 .... **22** C6
TOW NN12 .... **9** F6
Tower Crs *GTLIN* MK14 .... **37** K1 🔲
Tower Dr *GTLIN* MK14 .... **25** J6
Townsend Cl *RBEDW* MK43 .... **29** H5
Townsend Cottages
RMKS/WB MK17 .... **66** C2
Townsend Gv *BDWL* MK13 .... **24** E5
Trafalgar Av *BTCHLY* MK3 .... **61** H1
Tranlands Brigg *BDWL* MK13 .... **23** J3
Travell Ct *BDWL* MK13 .... **36** E4 🔲
Travis Gv *BTCHLY* MK3 .... **61** K3
Treborough *EMV/FZ* MK4.............. **61** G1
Tredington Gv *WTR/OFPK* MK7 ..... **51** G5
Tremayne Ct *EAG/OLD/WT* MK6 .... **49** K1
Trent Dr *NPAG* MK16 .... **26** C1
Trentishoe Crs *EMV/FZ* MK4 .... **49** G6
Trent Rd *BTCHLY* MK3 .... **61** H2
Tresham Ct *SHEN* MK5 .... **48** D2
Trevithick La *SHEN* MK5 .... **48** E4
Trevone Ct *EAG/OLD/WT* MK6 ... **49** K1 🔲
Trinity Rd *WOLV* MK12.................. **23** J6
Trispen Ct *EAG/OLD/WT* MK6 .... **3** J7
Troutbeck *EAG/OLD/WT* MK6........ **50** B1
Trubys Gdn *EAG/OLD/WT* MK6...... **49** K2
Trueman Pl *EAG/OLD/WT* MK6...... **49** J1
Trumpton La *WTR/OFPK* MK7 .... **51** H2
Tudeley Hale *WTR/OFPK* MK7 ... **51** G1 🔲
Tudor Gdns *STSTR* MK11............... **35** F3
Tuffnell Cl *WLLN* MK15 .... **26** D6 🔲
Tulla Ct *WEAT* MK2 .... **70** B1
Tummell Wy *WEAT* MK2 .... **62** B6
Tunbridge Gv *WTR/OFPK* MK7 ...... **51** F1
Turnberry Cl *BTCHLY* MK3 .... **61** F4
Turners Ms *GTLIN* MK14 .... **37** J1 🔲
Turnmill Av *EAG/OLD/WT* MK6...... **38** A4
Turnpike Rd *RMKS/WB* MK17......... **65** J1
Turpyn Ct *EAG/OLD/WT* MK6 ..... **50** C1 🔲
Tweedale Ct *RMKS/WB* MK17 .... **67** K6
Tweed Dr *BTCHLY* MK3 .... **61** G2
Twinflower *WTR/OFPK* MK7 ...... **51** G5 🔲
Twitchen La *EMV/FZ* MK4.............. **49** G6
Twitch Hl *TOW* NN12 .... **6** C1
Two Ridges Link
Grand Union Canal Wk
LBUZ LU7 .... **84** A3
Twyford La *WTR/OFPK* MK7 ...... **51** H4 🔲
Tylers Gn *BDWL* MK13 .... **2** C2
Tyne Sq *BTCHLY* MK3 .... **61** G2
Tyrell Cl *BUCK/WIN* MK18 .... **55** F4
Tyrells Gdns *RMKS/WB* MK17 .... **70** D5
Tyrells Rd *RMKS/WB* MK17 .... **70** D5
Tyrill *GTLIN* MK14 .... **25** F6
Tyrrell Wy *TOW* NN12 .... **5** F1
Tyson Pl *EAG/OLD/WT* MK6 .... **49** H1 🔲

U

Ullswater Dr *LBUZ* LU7 .... **83** H2
Ulverscroft *MKV* MK10 .... **39** F5
Ulyett Pl *EAG/OLD/WT* MK6 .... **49** H1
Underwood Pl *EAG/OLD/WT* MK6... **49** H1
Union St *NPAG* MK16 .... **16** C6 🔲
Upper Coombe *LBUZ* LU7 .... **83** K1 🔲
Upper Fifth St *CMK* MK9 .... **2** D5
Upper Second St *CMK* MK9 .... **2** B6
Upper Stonehayes *GTLIN* MK14 .. **25** J5 🔲
Upper Third St *CMK* MK9 .... **2** C5
Upper Wy *RMKS/WB* MK17............ **71** H4
Upton Gv *SHEN* MK5 .... **49** F5

V

Vache La *SHEN* MK5....................... **48** C3
Valens Cl *CNH/GTH/TM* MK8.......... **48** B2
Valentine Ct *CNH/GTH/TM* MK8..... **48** A2
Valerian Pl *NPAG* MK16 .... **25** J1
Valley Rd *BUCK/WIN* MK18 .... **55** J3
Van Der Bilt Ct *BDWL* MK13 ...... **36** C1 🔲
Vandyke Cl *RMKS/WB* MK17 .... **52** C3
Vandyke Rd *LBUZ* LU7 .... **84** C2
Vantage Ct *MKV* MK10 .... **26** C2
Vauxhall *BDWL* MK13 .... **36** E1
Venables La *WLLN* MK15................ **25** K6
Venetian Ct *WTR/OFPK* MK7 ...... **51** H2 🔲
Verdi Cl *WTR/OFPK* MK7 .... **51** J4 🔲
Verdon Dr *WLLN* MK15 .... **26** A6
Verity Pl *EAG/OLD/WT* MK6 .... **3** G7
Verley Cl *EAG/OLD/WT* MK6 .... **50** B1
Vermont Pl *WLLN* MK15 .... **26** B4
Verney Cl *BUCK/WIN* MK18............ **55** G2
Vernon Rd *TOW* NN12 .... **5** G4
Veryan Pl *EAG/OLD/WT* MK6 .... **3** K5
Vicarage Cl *TOW* NN12 .... **11** K5
Vicarage Gdns *BDWL* MK13 .... **36** D3 🔲
LBUZ LU7 .... **83** F3 🔲
Vicarage Rd *BDWL* MK13 .... **36** D3
BUCK/WIN MK18 .... **74** A3
LBUZ LU7 .... **83** F3 🔲
RMKS/WB MK17 .... **59** J3
STSTR MK11 .... **34** E1
WEAT MK2 .... **62** C3
Vicarage St *RMKS/WB* MK17 .... **52** D5
Vicarage Wk *STSTR* MK11............. **34** E1
Victoria Rd *LBUZ* LU7 .... **83** K3
WEAT MK2 .... **62** C3
Victoria St *WOLV* MK12 .... **36** A1
Vienna Gv *BDWL* MK13 .... **36** B1
Village Cl *NPAG* MK16 .... **16** E1
Villiers Cl *BUCK/WIN* MK18 .... **55** H1
Vimy Rd *LBUZ* LU7 .... **84** A2
Vincent Av *CNH/GTH/TM* MK8 .... **48** B2
Vintners Ms *GTLIN* MK14 .... **37** J1 🔟
Virginia *EAG/OLD/WT* MK6 .... **49** K2
Viscount Wy *WEAT* MK2 .... **62** B2
Vyne Crs *CNH/GTH/TM* MK8 .... **36** C6

W

Wadesmill La *WTR/OFPK* MK7 .... **51** G5
Wadhurst La *WTR/OFPK* MK7 .... **39** F6
Wagner Cl *WTR/OFPK* MK7 .... **51** H5
Wakefield Cl *GTLIN* MK14 .... **25** J6
Walbank Gv *SHEN* MK5 .... **48** C6
Walbrook Av *EAG/OLD/WT* MK6 .... **38** A4
Walgrave Dr *BDWL* MK13 .... **36** D4
Walkhampton Av *BDWL* MK13 .... **36** E4
Walk House Ct *RBEDW* MK43 .... **29** J4 🔲
The Walk *BUCK/WIN* MK18 .... **74** A4
Wallace St *BDWL* MK13 .... **24** B6
Wallinger Dr *SHEN* MK5 .... **48** D6
Wallingford *BDWL* MK13 .... **36** D2
Wallmead Gdns *SHEN* MK5............ **48** E2
Walney Pl *EMV/FZ* MK4.................. **60** C2
Walnut Cl *NPAG* MK16 .... **18** A1 🔲
TOW NN12 .... **18** A1 🔲
Walnut Dr *BUCK/WIN* MK18 .... **43** J5
WEAT MK2 .... **62** D3
The Walnuts *LBUZ* LU7 .... **80** B5 🔲
Walsh's Mnr *GTLIN* MK14 .... **25** G6
Waltham Dr *WTR/OFPK* MK7 .... **39** F6
Walton End *WTR/OFPK* MK7 .... **51** H3
Walton Heath *BTCHLY* MK3 .... **61** G3
Walton Rd *MKV* MK10 .... **38** E6
WTR/OFPK MK7 .... **51** J3
Wandlebury *GTLIN* MK14 .... **25** K5
Wandsworth Pl *BDWL* MK13 .... **2** C2
Wantage Crs *LBUZ* LU7 .... **82** D6
Warde Pl *EAG/OLD/WT* MK6 .... **49** H1
Ward Rd *DBGH* MK1 .... **50** C6
Warmington Gdns *WLLN* MK15...... **38** A2
Warners Cl *RMKS/WB* MK17 .... **71** H4
Warners Rd *RMKS/WB* MK17 .... **69** G2
Warren Cl *BUCK/WIN* MK18 .... **55** H4
Warren Rd *RMKS/WB* MK17 .... **59** G6
TOW NN12 .... **12** A5
Warwick Pl *BTCHLY* MK3 .... **61** H4
Warwick Rd *BTCHLY* MK3 .... **61** H4
Washfield *EMV/FZ* MK4 .... **49** G6
Washingleys *RBEDW* MK43 .... **29** K3 🔲
Wastel *EAG/OLD/WT* MK6.............. **50** A4
Watchcroft Dr *BUCK/WIN* MK18 .... **55** H1
Watchet Cl *EMV/FZ* MK4 .... **49** G6 🔲
Waterdell *LBUZ* LU7 .... **84** D2
Water Eaton Rd *BTCHLY* MK3 .... **62** A4

V

Waterhouse Cl *NPAG* MK16 ....
Water La *LBUZ* LU7 ....
NPAG MK16 ....
TOW NN12 ....
TOW NN12 ....
Waterloo Ct *BTCHLY* MK3 ....
Waterloo Rd *LBUZ* LU7 ....
Waterlow Cl *NPAG* MK16 ....
Waterside *EAG/OLD/WT* MK6 ....
Watermeet Cl *EMV/FZ* MK4 ....
Watery La *RMKN* MK19 ....
Watling St *BTCHLY* MK3 ....
CNH/GTH/TM MK8 ....
DBGH MK1 ....
EMV/FZ MK4 ....
SHEN MK5 ....
STSTR MK11 ....
WEAT MK2 ....
Watling Ter *WEAT* MK2 ....
Watlow Gdns *BUCK/WIN* MK18 ..
Wavell Cl *WLLN* MK15 ....
Wavendon House Dr
CNH/GTH/TM MK8 ....
Wavendon Rd *RMKS/WB* MK17...
Waveney Cl *NPAG* MK16................
Wealdstone Pl *EAG/OLD/WT* MK6
Weasel La *RMKS/WB* MK17 ....
Weathercock Cl *RMKS/WB* MK17
Weathercock La *RMKS/WB* MK17
Weavers End *RMKN* MK19 ....
Weavers Hl *STSTR* MK11 ....
Webber Heath *WTR/OFPK* MK7...
Websters Meadow
EMV/FZ MK4 ....
Wedgewood Av *GTLIN* MK14 ....
Wedgwood Av *GTLIN* MK14 ....
Welland Dr *NPAG* MK16................
Wellfield Ct *WLLN* MK15 ....
Wellhayes *GTLIN* MK14 ....
Wellington Pl *BTCHLY* MK3 ....
Well St *BUCK/WIN* MK18 ....
Wenning La *EMV/FZ* MK4...............
Wentworth Dr *LBUZ* LU7...............
Wentworth Wy *BTCHLY* MK3 ....
TOW NN12 ....
Werth Dr *RMKS/WB* MK17 ....
Westbrook End *RMKS/WB* MK17
Westbury Cl *NPAG* MK16................
Westbury La *NPAG* MK16 ....
Westcliffe *CNH/GTH/TM* MK8 ....
West Dales *BDWL* MK13 ....
Western Av *BUCK/WIN* MK18 ....
Western Rd *RMKS/WB* MK17 ....
WEAT MK2 ....
WOLV MK12 ....
Westfield Av *RMKN* MK19.............
Westfield Rd *WEAT* MK2 ....
Westfields *BUCK/WIN* MK18 ....
Westhill *GTLIN* MK14 ....
West Hl *RMKS/WB* MK17 ....
Westminster Dr *BTCHLY* MK3.........
West La *LBUZ* LU7 ....
West Rd *RBEDW* MK43 ....
RMKS/WB MK17 ....
West St *BUCK/WIN* MK18 ....
LBUZ LU7 ....
Westwood Cl *CNH/GTH/TM* MK8
Wetherby Gdns *BTCHLY* MK3 ....
Whaddon Rd *EMV/FZ* MK4.............
NPAG MK16 ....
RMKS/WB MK17 ....
RMKS/WB MK17 ....
SHEN MK5 ....
Whaddon Wy *BTCHLY* MK3 ....
Whalley Dr *BTCHLY* MK3 ....
Wharf La *RMKN* MK19 ....
Wharfside *WEAT* MK2 ....
Wharfside Pl *BUCK/WIN* MK18 ..
The Wharf *WEAT* MK2 ....
Wharf Vw *BUCK/WIN* MK18 ....
Wheatcroft Cl *EAG/OLD/WT* MK6
Wheatfield Cl *LBUZ* LU7 ....
Wheathouse Copse
RMKS/WB MK17 ....
Wheatley Cl *EMV/FZ* MK4..............
Wheelers La *BDWL* MK13 ....
Wheelwright Ms *GTLIN* MK14 ....
Whetstone Cl *BDWL* MK13 ....
Whichford *GTLIN* MK14..................
Whitby Cl *BTCHLY* MK3..................
White Alder *WOLV* MK12...............
Whitebaker Ct *GTLIN* MK14 ....
Whitegate Ct
EAG/OLD/WT MK6 ....
Whitehall Av *MKV* MK10 ....
White Horse Ct *LBUZ* LU7 ....
White Horse Dr *EMV/FZ* MK4 ....
Whiteley Crs *BTCHLY* MK3 ....

orns *NPAC* MK16 .... **26** A2
 Pasture *WLLN* MK15 ... **26** A6 ▣
ury Ct *TOW* NN12............. **9** F6
ury Rd *TOW* NN12............. **8** B6
s La *TOW* NN12................. **5** F3
 Wy *NPAG* MK16............... **26** B2
th La *SHEN* MK5............... **48** E2
Park Rd *RMKN* MK19......... **45** G1
Rd *BUCK/WIN* MK18......... **44** D1
 Gdns *RMKS/WB* MK17 ... **66** B3
e Rd *SHEN* MK5................. **48** C5
Cl *WLLN* MK15.................. **38** B5
a *GTLIN* MK14................... **25** J5
ark Av *WLLN* MK15......... **26** A6
d *MKV* MK10...................... **38** E4
a *SHEN* MK5..................... **26** C2
'i *SHEN* MK5..................... **48** D4
Bandy *LBUZ* LU7 .... **82** E6 ▣
Cir *WTR/OFPK* MK7 .. **51** F5 ▣
Smith Cl *WLLN* MK15...... **38** B4
 TOW NN12....................... **5** F4
ank Wk *LBUZ* LU7........... **84** D1
l *NPAC* MK16.................... **27** K5
N12 .... **5** F5
r *BUCK/WIN* MK18 .... **55** J4
ord *BDWL* MK13............. **36** B2
Park *RMKN* MK19........... **34** C1
d *RMKS/WB* MK17......... **66** B2
prings *RBEDW* MK43 .... **29** H5
y *LBUZ* LU7..................... **82** D6
 MK2................................. **62** B4
av *SHEN* MK5.................. **48** E2
ound *WTR/OFPK* MK7 .. **51** G1 ▣
st *CNH/GTH/TM* MK8 .. **48** B2 ▣
BTCHLY MK3.................. **61** K3
on Pl *BDWL* MK13............ **2** B3
e Crs *EMV/FZ* MK4......... **60** C1
on Hl *BTCHLY* MK3......... **61** F5

Winchester Cir *MKV* MK10 .... **39** H6
Windermere Dr *WEAT* MK2 .... **62** C6
Windermere Gdns *LBUZ* LU7 ...... **83** H2 ▣
Windmill Cl *BUCK/WIN* MK18 ..... **55** J2
Windmill Hill Dr *BTCHLY* MK3 .... **61** F4
Windmill Pth *LBUZ* LU7 .... **84** B2 ▣
Windmill Wy *RBEDW* MK43 .... **29** K3 ▣
 TOW NN12 .... **4** A1
Windsor Av *LBUZ* LU7 .... **84** A2
 NPAG MK16 .... **26** B1
Windsor Cl *TOW* NN12 .... **4** E5
Windsor St *WEAT* MK2 .... **62** B3
 WOLV MK12 .... **35** K1
Winfold La *EMV/FZ* MK4 .... **60** E2
Wingate Cir *WTR/OFPK* MK7 .. **51** F5 ▣
Wingfield Gv *MKV* MK10............. **39** F5
Wing Rd *LBUZ* LU7 .... **83** K2 ▣
Winsford Hl *EMV/FZ* MK4 .... **49** H6
Winslow Rd *RMKS/WB* MK17 ...... **58** D4
 RMKS/WB MK17 .... **66** E4
 RMKS/WB MK17 .... **75** H4
Winstanley La *SHEN* MK5 .... **49** F5
Winston Cl *LBUZ* LU7.................. **80** B6
Winterburn *BDWL* MK13.............. **36** E2
Wisewood Rd *EMV/FZ* MK4 .... **48** A5
Wishart Gn *WTR/OFPK* MK7 .... **51** K4
Wistmans *EMV/FZ* MK4................ **49** G5
Witan Ct *CMK* MK9 .... **2** C5
Witan Ga *CMK* MK9 .... **2** C5
Witham Ct *BTCHLY* MK3 .... **61** G2
Withington *BDWL* MK13 .... **36** D2
Withycombe *EMV/FZ* MK4 .... **49** H6
Wittmills Oak *BUCK/WIN* MK18 ... **55** H2
Woad La *GTLIN* MK14................... **25** H5
Woburn Av *WOLV* MK12 .... **35** J1
Woburn Gn *RMKS/WB* MK17 .... **53** F6
Woburn Pl *LBUZ* LU7 .... **80** B6 ▣
Woburn Rd *LBUZ* LU7 .... **80** B1

 RMKS/WB MK17 .... **63** K5
 RMKS/WB MK17 .... **64** D1
Woburn Sands Rd
 RMKS/WB MK17 .... **63** J1
Wolfscote La *EMV/FZ* MK4 .... **48** E6
Wolsey Gdns *BDWL* MK13........... **36** D3
Wolverton Rd *GTLIN* MK14 .... **25** G4
 NPAC MK16 .... **26** A1
 RMKN MK19 .... **13** K6
 RMKN MK19 .... **24** A3
 STSTR MK11 .... **35** F2
Woodcroft Cl *TOW* NN12 .... **5** F6 ▣
Wood End *RBEDW* MK43 .... **41** J1
 RMKS/WB MK17 .... **67** F3
Wood End La *NPAC* MK16............ **27** K4
Woodhouse Ct *GTLIN* MK14 .... **37** F1
Woodland Av *LBUZ* LU7.............. **80** A5
Woodlands Cl *BUCK/WIN* MK18.... **55** C1
Woodlands Crs
 BUCK/WIN MK18 .... **55** G1 ▣
The Woodlands *TOW* NN12 ...... **18** A1 ▣
Woodland Vw *WOLV* MK12........... **36** A2
Woodland Wy *RMKS/WB* MK17 ... **52** C6
Wood La *GTLIN* MK14.................. **25** H6
 RMKS/WB MK17 .... **52** E6
Woodley Headland
 EAG/OLD/WT MK6........................ **50** B2
Woodman Cl *LBUZ* LU7............... **82** E6
 LBUZ LU7 .... **84** C2
Woodruff Av *GTLIN* MK14 .... **2** D1
Woodrush Cl *EAG/OLD/WT* MK6 ... **50** A5
Woodside *RMKS/WB* MK17 .... **52** E5
 STSTR MK11 .... **35** F4
Woodside Wy *LBUZ* LU7 .... **83** J3 ▣
Woods La *TOW* NN12 .... **21** K2
Woodstock Ct *BDWL* MK13 .... **24** E6
Wood St *BDWL* MK13................... **24** C6
 RMKS/WB MK17 .... **52** C5

The Wood *LBUZ* LU7 .... **84** B1
Woodville Crs *TOW* NN12 ...... **11** K5 ▣
Woodward Pl *CNH/GTH/TM* MK8 .. **36** D6
Woolmans *STSTR* MK11.............. **35** H3
Woolrich Gdns *STSTR* MK11....... **35** F2
Worcester Cl *NPAG* MK16 .... **25** J1
Wordsworth Av *NPAC* MK16 .... **15** J6
Wordsworth Cl *TOW* NN12.......... **4** D4
Wordsworth Dr *BTCHLY* MK3...... **61** K4
Worrelle Av *MKV* MK10............... **38** E4
Wray Ct *EMV/FZ* MK4 .... **60** D1
Wren Cl *BUCK/WIN* MK18 ...... **55** J4 ▣
 TOW NN12 .... **5** F6
Wrens Pk *MKV* MK10................... **39** F5
Wyblington Dr *EAG/OLD/WT* MK6.. **49** K5
Wye Cl *BTCHLY* MK3................... **61** F2
Wylie End *BDWL* MK13................ **24** D6
Wymondham *WTR/OFPK* MK7...... **39** G6
Wyness Av *RMKS/WB* MK17 .... **63** K6
Wyngates *LBUZ* LU7 .... **83** K4
Wynyard Ct *EAG/OLD/WT* MK6 ... **49** H2

Y

Yalts Brow *EMV/FZ* MK4.............. **60** E1
Yardley Rd *RMKN* MK19 .... **22** D3
 TOW NN12 .... **21** K1
Yarrow Pl *GTLIN* MK14 .... **37** H3
Yeats Cl *NPAC* MK16 .... **15** J6
Yeomans Dr *GTLIN* MK14 .... **25** K5
Yew Tree Cl *RMKS/WB* MK17 ...... **69** F2
Yonder Slade *BUCK/WIN* MK18 ... **55** G5
York Cl *TOW* NN12 .... **5** F5
York Rd *STSTR* MK11................... **34** E2

Index - featured places

Combined School
 LY MK3 .... **61** K1
Vood Junior School
 W MK19............................. **33** F6
Vood School
 /WIN MK18........................ **43** F2
mpbell County
 e School
 LY MK3 .... **61** G4
k County First School
 GTH/TM MK8 .... **36** B6
 Surgery
 LU7 .... **82** D6
s Medical Centre
 /WB MK17 .... **52** C5
uise Golf Club & Shop
 /WB MK17 .... **52** E5
uise Primary School
 /WB MK17 .... **53** G5
usiness Centre
 MK1 .... **62** A1
ert Lower School
 LU7 .... **84** E1
shire County Council
 LU7 .... **84** B3
rker RC School
 MK2 .... **62** B5
 Leisure Centre
 MK2 .... **62** C3
 Meadow
ty Combined School
 /WIN MK18 .... **55** J3
l Priory
 . MK13................................ **36** C3
Village County
 e School
 . MK13................................ **36** E3
nds Middle School
 LU7..................................... **84** D3
ham
 munity Hospital
 /WIN MK18 .... **55** G2
ham Golf Club
 /WIN MK18 .... **54** C4
ham Middle School
 /WIN MK18 .... **55** H1
ham Rugby
 n Football Club
 /WIN MK18 .... **43** H5
ham School
 /WIN MK18 .... **55** G4
hamshire
 ty Council
 OLD/WT MK6 .... **50** A3
hamshire
 ty Council
 MK16 .... **25** J1

Buckingham Town Council
 BUCK/WIN MK18.................... **55** G2
Buckingham Town
 Football Club
 BUCK/WIN MK18.................... **55** G3
Buckingham University
 BUCK/WIN MK18.................... **55** F3
Bury Lawn School
 GTLIN MK14 .... **25** G6
Bushfield County Middle School
 WOLV MK12 .... **36** A1
Canal Museum
 TOW NN12............................. **7** F1
Caroline Haslett County
 Combined School
 SHEN MK5 .... **48** E5
The Carpet Gallery
 WEAT MK2 .... **62** B3
Castles County First School
 BTCHLY MK3 .... **61** H4
Castlethorpe First School
 RMKN MK19........................... **13** G5
Cedars County
 Combined School
 NPAC MK16 .... **26** C1
Cedars Upper School &
 Community College
 LBUZ LU7............................. **83** K4
Central Milton Keynes
 Medical Centre
 CMK MK9 .... **2** D4
Chackmore C of E First School
 BUCK/WIN MK18.................... **42** E5
Chammandean School
 BUCK/WIN MK18.................... **30** E3
Cherrycourt Way
 Industrial Estate
 LBUZ LU7............................. **84** E3
Cherrycourt Way Trading Estate
 LBUZ LU7............................. **85** F3
Chiltern Trading Estate
 LBUZ LU7............................. **84** B4
Church of Christ the Cornerstone
 CMK MK9 .... **2** E4
Church of England School
 BUCK/WIN MK18.................... **43** J1
Church of England School
 RMKS/WB MK17 .... **76** A1
Clinic/nutri-centre
 NPAC MK16 .... **16** C6
Clipstone Brook Industrial Park
 LBUZ LU7............................. **84** E3
Clipstone Brook School
 LBUZ LU7............................. **84** C2
Club House
 RBEDW MK43 .... **41** K6

Cold Harbour C of E
 Combined School
 BTCHLY MK3 .... **49** J6
Combined School
 BDWL MK13.......................... **24** C6
Commerce Way
 Industrial Estate
 LBUZ LU7............................. **85** F3
Conniburrow Middle School
 GTLIN MK14 .... **37** H2
Copperfield Middle School
 EAG/OLD/WT MK6 .... **49** K4
Cornhill County First School
 EAG/OLD/WT MK6 .... **49** K3
Cosgrove Leisure Park
 RMKN MK19........................... **23** H3
Cosgrove Primary School
 RMKN MK19........................... **23** F3
Council Offices
 TOW NN12............................. **4** D4
County First School
 GTLIN MK14 .... **25** J6
County Middle School
 BUCK/WIN MK18.................... **55** G4
County Middle School
 GTLIN MK14 .... **25** J6
County Primary School
 RMKN MK19........................... **22** C6
Cranfield Lower School
 RBEDW MK43 .... **29** J4
Cranfield University
 BTCHLY MK3 .... **62** A2
Cranfield University
 RBEDW MK43 .... **29** F3
Cromwell Business Centre
 NPAC MK16 .... **26** E2
Deanshanger Primary School
 RMKN MK19........................... **33** K4
De Montfort University
 WTR/OFPK MK7 .... **51** F2
Denbigh Hall Industrial Estate
 BTCHLY MK3 .... **49** J5
Denbigh Industrial Estate
 DBGH MK1 .... **62** B1
Denbigh School
 SHEN MK5 .... **48** D3
Dovery Down CP School
 LBUZ LU7............................. **80** B5
Downsbarn County First School
 GTLIN MK14 .... **37** J2
Dragon Gallery
 BUCK/WIN MK18.................... **55** F2
Drayton Park Combined School
 WEAT MK2 .... **62** B6
Drayton Parslow First School
 RMKS/WB MK17 .... **76** E1
Drayton Road Surgery
 WEAT MK2 .... **62** C5

Eaglestone Health Centre
 EAG/OLD/WT MK6 .... **50** A2
Eaton Mill County
 Combined School
 WEAT MK2 .... **62** C5
Emerson Valley
 Combined School
 EMV/FZ MK4 .... **61** F1
Entertainment Centre
 CMK MK9 .... **3** J4
Europa Business Park
 MKV MK10............................ **39** J5
Falconhurst County
 Combined School
 EAG/OLD/WT MK6 .... **50** A1
Falcon Manor School
 TOW NN12............................. **4** A1
Fenny Lodge Gallery
 DBGH MK1 .... **62** D1
Fernwood School
 RMKS/WB MK17 .... **64** C1
Fishermead Medical Centre
 EAG/OLD/WT MK6 .... **3** H6
Friends Meeting House
 GTLIN MK14 .... **2** D1
Fulbrook Secondary School
 RMKS/WB MK17 .... **52** C4
Gayhurst House
 NPAG MK16 .... **15** G2
Germander Park
 County First School
 GTLIN MK14 .... **2** D1
Giffard Park County
 Combined School
 GTLIN MK14 .... **25** K3
Gilbert Inglefield Middle School
 LBUZ LU7............................. **80** D6
Glastonbury Thorne
 First School
 SHEN MK5 .... **48** D3
Grafton Medical Centre
 CMK MK9 .... **2** B5
Great Brickhill Cricket Club
 RMKS/WB MK17 .... **71** H3
Great Horwood School
 RMKS/WB MK17 .... **66** A2
Great Linford County Combined
 School
 GTLIN MK14 .... **25** H5
Greaves Way Industrial Estate
 LBUZ LU7............................. **84** E3
Greenleas Lower School
 LBUZ LU7............................. **83** G2
Greenleys County
 Middle School
 WOLV MK12 .... **35** K2

Green Park County
Combined School
NPAG MK16 .... 26 A2
Greens Norton C of E
Primary School
TOW NN12 .... 4 B1
The Grove Independent School
SHEN MK5 .... 49 F2
Grover Surgery
EAG/OLD/WT MK6 .... 50 A3
The Grove Surgery
EAG/OLD/WT MK6 .... 50 A3
Gyosei International School
WLLN MK15 .... 38 B2
Harmill Industrial Estate
LBUZ LU7 .... 84 B4
Haversham Manor
RMKN MK19 .... 24 C3
Heathwood CP School
LBUZ LU7 .... 80 C4
Heelands County First School
BDWL MK13 .... 36 E3
Heronsgate Combined School
WTR/OFPK MK7 .... 51 G4
High Ash C of E
Combined School
RMKS/WB MK17 .... 71 J3
Hilltops Medical Centre
CNH/GTH/TM MK8 .... 36 C6
HM Prison Milton Keynes
EMV/FZ MK4 .... 48 A5
Holmwood First School
CNH/GTH/TM MK8 .... 36 B6
Holne Chase Combined School
BTCHLY MK3 .... 61 K4
Holywell Middle School
RBEDW MK43 .... 29 J4
Horn Street Surgery
BUCK/WIN MK18 .... 74 A3
Husborne Crawley
Lower School
RBEDW MK43 .... 53 K5
John Hellins Primary School
TOW NN12 .... 21 J2
Kart Circuit
BDWL MK13 .... 36 D5
Kents Hill First School
WTR/OFPK MK7 .... 51 F2
Kiln Farm Industrial Estate
STSTR MK11 .... 35 J4
Kingfisher Golf & Country Club
RMKN MK19 .... 34 B5
Kingfisher Surgery
NPAG MK16 .... 26 B2
Kingsbrook School
RMKN MK19 .... 34 A3
Knowles County First &
Middle School
WEAT MK2 .... 62 C3
Langland County Combined
School
EAG/OLD/WT MK6 .... 50 B3
Leedon CP Infant School
LBUZ LU7 .... 84 D3
Leighton Buzzard Theatre
LBUZ LU7 .... 84 B2
Leighton Linslade
Town Council
LBUZ LU7 .... 84 B2
Leighton Middle School
LBUZ LU7 .... 84 A3
Leisure Plaza
CMK MK9 .... 49 F1
Leon School
WEAT MK2 .... 62 B6
Linslade Lower School
LBUZ LU7 .... 83 J2
Linslade Middle School
LBUZ LU7 .... 83 K4
Lodge Farm Industrial Estate
RMKN MK19 .... 23 J2
Lodge Industrial Centre
RMKS/WB MK17 .... 77 F1
Lord Grey School
BTCHLY MK3 .... 61 J2
Loughton County
Middle School
SHEN MK5 .... 48 D2
Loughton Manor First School
SHEN MK5 .... 48 D1
Lovat Middle School
NPAG MK16 .... 26 C2
Maids Moreton C of E
First School
BUCK/WIN MK18 .... 43 H6
Mary Bassett School
LBUZ LU7 .... 84 A2
Maryland College
RMKS/WB MK17 .... 65 F5
Masonic House Surgery
BUCK/WIN MK18 .... 55 G2
The Meacham Clinic
WOLV MK12 .... 23 J6
Middleton Swimming Pool
NPAG MK16 .... 26 D2

Milton Keynes Borough Council
CMK MK9 .... 3 F2
Milton Keynes Central Business
Exchange
CMK MK9 .... 2 E5
Milton Keynes College
BTCHLY MK3 .... 62 A3
Milton Keynes College
EAG/OLD/WT MK6 .... 49 J2
Milton Keynes Council
CMK MK9 .... 3 F3
Milton Keynes Council
WEAT MK2 .... 62 B3
Milton Keynes Gallery
CMK MK9 .... 3 H3
Milton Keynes Hospital
EAG/OLD/WT MK6 .... 50 A2
Milton Keynes
Museum of Industry &
Rural Life
WOLV MK12 .... 36 B2
Milton Keynes
Preparatory School
BTCHLY MK3 .... 61 G3
Milton Keynes
Preparatory School
NPAG MK16 .... 39 G3
Milton Keynes Rugby Club
WOLV MK12 .... 35 J2
Milton Keynes Theatre
CMK MK9 .... 3 H3
Milton Keynes Village Practice
MKV MK10 .... 39 F4
Milton Medical Centre
WEAT MK2 .... 62 B3
M K Stadium
EAG/OLD/WT MK6 .... 50 B5
Moorland County First School
EAG/OLD/WT MK6 .... 50 A4
National Badminton Centre
CNH/GTH/TM MK8 .... 36 D5
National Hockey Stadium
CMK MK9 .... 2 A5
Neath Hill Health Centre
GTLIN MK14 .... 25 J6
New Bradwell Mosque
BDWL MK13 .... 24 D6
Newlyn Place First School
EAG/OLD/WT MK6 .... 3 K5
Newport Pagnell
County Council
NPAG MK16 .... 16 B6
Newport Pagnell
Medical Centre
NPAG MK16 .... 26 B1
Nicholas Hawksmoor
Primary School
TOW NN12 .... 4 E4
Oldbrook County First School
EAG/OLD/WT MK6 .... 49 H1
The Old Church School
BTCHLY MK3 .... 61 J4
Open Air Theatre
CMK MK9 .... 3 K2
Open University
DBGH MK1 .... 62 D1
The Open University
DBGH MK1 .... 50 D6
The Open University
STSTR MK11 .... 34 E2
The Open University
WTR/OFPK MK7 .... 50 E2
Ousedale School
NPAG MK16 .... 26 A2
Page Hill First School
BUCK/WIN MK18 .... 55 H1
Pages Industrial Park
LBUZ LU7 .... 84 C4
Pepper Hill County First School
BDWL MK13 .... 24 D6
The Place Retail Park
CMK MK9 .... 36 E6
The Point Entertainment Centre
CMK MK9 .... 3 F4
Police HQ
CMK MK9 .... 2 C4
Portfields Combined School
NPAG MK16 .... 15 K6
Potterspury Lodge School
TOW NN12 .... 11 F5
Pulford VA Lower School
LBUZ LU7 .... 84 A3
Queensway Clinic
WEAT MK2 .... 62 C3
Radcliffe School
WOLV MK12 .... 35 J1
Redhouse Surgery
WEAT MK2 .... 62 C3
Redway School
EAG/OLD/WT MK6 .... 50 B2
Retail Park
BDWL MK13 .... 36 E5

Retail Park
CMK MK9 .... 49 F1
Rickley County Middle School
BTCHLY MK3 .... 61 J3
Riding School
BUCK/WIN MK18 .... 42 B2
Rivers County First School
BTCHLY MK3 .... 61 H3
Riverside County First School
NPAG MK16 .... 26 D2
Romans Field School
BTCHLY MK3 .... 61 H2
Rooksley Trading E state
BDWL MK13 .... 36 E5
Royal Latin School
BUCK/WIN MK18 .... 55 G4
St Andrews C of E First School
GTLIN MK14 .... 25 H4
St Georges Lower School
LBUZ LU7 .... 84 C1
St Lawrence School
TOW NN12 .... 5 F4
St Leonards Heath &
Reach VA Lower School
LBUZ LU7 .... 80 B2
St Mary Magdalene RC
Combined School
WOLV MK12 .... 35 H2
St Michaels C of E
Combined School
LBUZ LU7 .... 77 G6
St Monicas School
GTLIN MK14 .... 37 J1
St Pauls RC Secondary School
EAG/OLD/WT MK6 .... 49 J2
St Thomas Aquinas
RC Combined School
BTCHLY MK3 .... 61 H4
Saxon Clinic
EAG/OLD/WT MK6 .... 50 A2
School House
WLLN MK15 .... 24 C6
Sewage Works
WLLN MK15 .... 38 E1
Shenley Brook End School
BTCHLY MK3 .... 61 K2
Shenley Brook End School
SHEN MK5 .... 48 D6
Shenley Leisure Centre
SHEN MK5 .... 48 C2
Shepherdswell County
First School
EAG/OLD/WT MK6 .... 38 A5
Sherington School
NPAG MK16 .... 17 F1
Shopping Centre
CMK MK9 .... 2 E4
Silson Surgery
TOW NN12 .... 8 A6
Silverstone C of E
Junior School
TOW NN12 .... 18 A1
Silverstone
Motor Racing Circuit
TOW NN12 .... 18 C4
Simpson County
Combined School
EAG/OLD/WT MK6 .... 50 C4
Sir Frank Markham
Community School
EAG/OLD/WT MK6 .... 49 J2
South Beds District Council
LBUZ LU7 .... 84 A1
Southcott Lower School
LBUZ LU7 .... 83 J2
Sovereign Medical Centre
GTLIN MK14 .... 25 K6
Spinney Park Industrial Estate
LBUZ LU7 .... 84 C5
Sponne House Shopping Centre
TOW NN12 .... 5 F3
Sponne School
TOW NN12 .... 4 E3
Sports Centre
TOW NN12 .... 4 E4
Stantonbury Health Centre
GTLIN MK14 .... 25 F6
Stanton County Middle School
BDWL MK13 .... 24 E6
Station Road Industrial Estate
BUCK/WIN MK18 .... 74 B2
Stoke Bruerne C of E
Primary School
TOW NN12 .... 7 F1
Stony Stratford Health Centre
STSTR MK11 .... 34 E2
Stony Stratford Sports Club
STSTR MK11 .... 34 E1
Stowe Castle Business Park
BUCK/WIN MK18 .... 42 E2
Stowe School
BUCK/WIN MK18 .... 42 B2

Summerfield County
Combined School
BDWL MK13 ....
Sutherlands School
LBUZ LU7 ....
Swallowfield Lower School
RMKS/WB MK17 ....
Swanbourne C of E
Aidded School
RMKS/WB MK17 ....
The Swan Pool & Leisure Centre
BUCK/WIN MK18 ....
Technology Park
RBEDW MK43 ....
Thornborough First School
BUCK/WIN MK18 ....
Tickford Abbey
NPAG MK16 ....
Tiddenfoot Leisure Centre
LBUZ LU7 ....
Towcester Health Centre
TOW NN12 ....
Towcester Infant School
TOW NN12 ....
Towcester Medical Centre
TOW NN12 ....
Towcester Town F C
TOW NN12 ....
Towcestrians Sports Club
TOW NN12 ....
Two Mile Ash Middle School
CNH/GTH/TM MK8 ....
Tyringham Health Clinic
NPAG MK16 ....
Vale of Aylesbury
District Council
BUCK/WIN MK18 ....
Vandyke Upper School &
Community College
LBUZ LU7 ....
Verney Close Family Practice
BUCK/WIN MK18 ....
Walnut Tree Health Centre
WTR/OFPK MK7 ....
Water Eaton Health Centre
WEAT MK2 ....
Water Hall Combined School
WEAT MK2 ....
Watling Vale Medical Centre
SHEN MK5 ....
Watling Way Middle School
STSTR MK11 ....
Wavendon First School
RMKS/WB MK17 ....
Wellsmead County First School
BTCHLY MK3 ....
Wellsmead County
Middle School
BTCHLY MK3 ....
Whaddon Primary School
RMKS/WB MK17 ....
Whalley Drive Child Health Clinic
BTCHLY MK3 ....
White Spire School
BTCHLY MK3 ....
Whittlebury C of E
Primary School
TOW NN12 ....
Willen County Combined School
WLLN MK15 ....
Willen Village Surgery
WLLN MK15 ....
Windmill
BDWL MK13 ....
Windmill Hill Golf Club
BTCHLY MK3 ....
Winslow C of E
Combined School
BUCK/WIN MK18 ....
Woburn Golf & Country Club
RMKS/WB MK17 ....
Woburn Lower School
RMKS/WB MK17 ....
Wolverton Health
Centre & Day Hospital
WOLV MK12 ....
Wolverton Sports Club
WOLV MK12 ....
Woodburcote Way
Industrial Estate
TOW NN12 ....
Wyvern County First School
WOLV MK12 ....
Xscape Ski, Leisure &
Entertainment Centre
CMK MK9 ....
Yardley Gobion C of E
Primary School
TOW NN12 ....
YMCA
CMK MK9 ....
Youngs Industrial Estate
LBUZ LU7 ....

Notes